New Architects 3

New Architects 3

The Architecture Foundation presents Britain's best emerging practices: 31/44 Architects . A449 . ACME . Adam Khan Architects . Adam Nathaniel Furman . Amin Taha . AOC . Archipelago . Architecture 00 . Article 25 . Asif Khan . Assemble . AY Architects . Baxendale Design Co . Bell Phillips . Carl Trenfield Architects . Carl Turner Architects . Carmody Groarke . CarverHaggard . Casper Mueller Kneer . Cassion Castle Architects . Citizens Design Bureau . Civic Architects . Coffey Architects . Coombs Jones . Dallas Pierce Quintero . David Kohn Architects . Delvendahl Martin . Denizen Works . DK-CM . Dominic McKenzie Architects . Duggan Morris . Dyvik Kahlen . Emulsion . Erect Architecture . Feilden Fowles . Friend and Company . Gatti Routh Rhodes . Gort Scott . Graeme Massie Architects . Hall McKnight . Haptic . HAT Projects . Hayhurst and Co . Hugh Strange Architects . Hugo Hardy . Invisible Studio . Jack Woolley . Jan Kattein Architects . Jonathan Hendry Architects . Laura Dewe Mathews . Liddicoat & Goldhill . Lyndon Goode Architects . Matheson Whiteley . Mikhail Riches . MW Architects . Nex . Nissen Richards . OMMX . Ordinary Architecture . Orkidstudio . OS31 . Platform 5 Architects . Practice Architecture . Prewett Bizley . Pricegore . PUP . RA Projects . RCKa . Robin Lee Architecture . Roz Barr Architects . Rural Office for Architecture . Russian for Fish . Sam Jacob Studio . Sandy Rendel Architects . Serie . Something & Son . Stitch . Studio Egret West . Studio Gil . Studio Sam Causer . Studio Weave . Surman Weston . Takero Shimazaki Architects . TDO . The Klassnik Corporation . Timothy Smith and Jonathan Taylor . Urban Projects Bureau . vPPR . We Made That . West Architecture . William Matthews Associates . William Smalley . YOU & ME

MERRELL
LONDON · NEW YORK

The
Architecture
Foundation

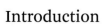
Introduction

There are several reasons why I am delighted to write the foreword to this third edition of 'New Architects'. First, because I was one of the Architecture Foundation's founders in 1991 and it is gratifying to see it continue to do good works in the cause of architecture – now under the direction of Ellis Woodman. Second, because the publication has an excellent tradition of spotting talent. So many of the 'young architects' featured in the first edition are now established names – David Adjaye, Allford Hall Monaghan Morris, Walters & Cohen, Sergison Bates, Sarah Wigglesworth, Terry Pawson, Keith Williams and Ian Simpson to name just some. Finally, I believe passionately in promoting young architects and designers to enable them to fulfil their promise.

From time to time my advice is sought by younger colleagues about whether they should make the leap and start up in practice on their own account. They are always guaranteed a sympathetic ear and in every case I have encouraged them to do so. Sometimes, to make a point in these conversations, I relate back to my own past. For example, I talk about the role of those who commission works from young practices and the importance of being grateful for their trust.

Recently my wife organised a surprise party to mark my birthday and invited a wide cross-section of people, who each in their different ways had touched my life. One was Fred Olsen for whom we had realised our first project in the late nineteen sixties – an operations centre in London's Docklands – which has since evolved into Canary Wharf. He said that he regretted not building the other projects that we had designed for him in Norway and the Canary Islands. It caused me to reflect on these and all the others of that time that were similarly unrealised. Because we had put our hearts and souls into these designs they have endured beyond the disappointments of that time and proved to be models for later development.

I can now see many of our subsequent projects, built decades later, are rooted in the idealism and principles that were founded in those early years. Masdar, our eco-city in the desert, for example, is in the footsteps of the Olsen project for Gomera in the Canaries. Our 1971 IBM Headquarters at Cosham was a built realisation of the Newport school design. The lesson is that nothing is wasted – in the longterm every exploration has a value, even if it may not be apparent at the time. Early failures often contain the seeds for future success.

So whatever the outcome might be, I would say that when the time feels right you will be richer for having made the move into that category of being one of the 'New Architects'. I wish you every success in that endeavour.

Norman Foster, Chairman and Founder Foster + Partners

Celebrating the work of close to 100 architectural practices that have established themselves in the UK since 2005, New Architects 3 is the latest addition to a series of publications that the Architecture Foundation launched in 1998. Serving as guides for potential clients, the books were conceived in response to a comment by the then Secretary of State for the Environment, John Gummer, that the vast majority of lottery-funded projects were going 'to architects over sixty'. Previous volumes have proved hugely effective in expanding the opportunities available to the selected practices, but the UK's culture of architectural patronage remains notably more risk-averse than that of many countries in continental Europe.

The challenges faced by the practices included in the present volume have been compounded by the contraction in the UK economy that followed the 2008 banking crisis. The downturn hit the construction sector particularly hard, leading to 378 architectural practices being declared insolvent in the two years from April 2011 alone.[1] Reductions in public sector capital investment and an ongoing failure to address the UK's long-standing housing crisis have ensured that conditions faced by British architects remain far from sympathetic. As the relatively small number of regional firms included in this volume testifies, this is particularly true for those based outside London.

However, if the New Architects 3 generation has undergone a baptism of fire, the experience has proved a spur to both its entrepreneurialism and artistic creativity. The work included in this book contrasts with that gathered in previous editions of the series in a number of key respects. Particularly striking is its geographic spread. The number of projects for overseas locations has increased five-fold in relation to the last volume. They include schemes designed for sites elsewhere in Europe but also for the burgeoning markets of China, India and Singapore. Frequently these are of

Adam Nathaniel Furman is one of many architects included in New Architects 3 whose work extends beyond established disciplinary boundaries. He is shown here with Identity Parade, a family of 3D-printed objects, which he produced in the course of a residency at the Design Museum.

The first project undertaken by Assemble was the Cineroleum, a temporary cinema created through the remodelling of a disused petrol station in London's Clerkenwell.

a scale that dwarfs the built work that their architects have been able to realise in the UK. Encountering a paucity of opportunity at home, many among this generation are pursuing their fortunes elsewhere.

Equally notable is the new freedom with which they are interpreting the architect's role. Few of the selected practices restrict themselves to commissions of a conventionally architectural scale. New Architects 3 features designs for masterplans; landscapes; play-areas; furniture; products; exhibitions; street signage; theatre sets; temporary pavilions for retail, dining and performance; not to mention myriad, less-readily-classifiable commissions that extend into the territory of art practice.

One firm whose work exemplifies this expanded definition of practice particularly vividly is the fourteen-member collective, Assemble. Focused on a core group who completed their degrees in architecture at the University of Cambridge in 2008, its membership includes artists, designers and others educated in entirely non-visual disciplines. They came together in 2009, with an ambition to build – the architecture graduates among them admitting to frustration at the slow pace of delivery that they encountered as year-out students. Lacking funds, they knew any project would have to cover its costs, but were determined that it should be more than a mere commercial proposition. They wanted to make something of public worth.

The result was the Cineroleum, a cinema that operated for three weeks that summer under the canopy of a disused petrol station in London's Clerkenwell. Funded by ticket and drink sales, constructed in large part from salvaged materials and built by a workforce of more than 50 volunteers, the project was imbued with a glamour that belied its low-cost origins. The iconography of the golden age of cinema-going was brought to bear on the materials of the builders' yard: drop-down seats constructed from reclaimed softwood planks, an encompassing black-out curtain made from yards of Tyvek. Six years on, Assemble is now undertaking substantial built commissions, but continues to challenge the established definitions of architectural practice. While yet to secure professional accreditation from the Architects Registration Board, the firm was the recipient of the 2015 Turner Prize, the UK's most prestigious award for contemporary art.

Architecture 00, also featured in these pages, run an equally unconventional model, their award-winning architectural practice forming one of a family of related operations. These include WikiHouse and OpenDesk, which offer open-sourced designs – at the scale, respectively, of building and furniture – suitable for digital download and local fabrication in timber. The practice was also instrumental in the formation of the Impact Hub Network, an organization now operating 73 incubator spaces for small businesses in 49 countries, and has led research on the civic economy for the innovation charity, Nesta. In The Foundry, a flexible workspace for not-for-profit organisations working in the field of social justice and human rights, the practice has realised its most substantial building to date, strongly informed by its wider research activities.

At a time of limited building, diversification makes good business sense. Yet the new generation's interest in challenging received disciplinary boundaries speaks of more than commercial opportunism: it reflects their frustration at the increasingly meager contribution that mainstream practice is permitted to make to the common good.

Their efforts to reclaim a role for architecture as the embodiment of a civic society are also informed by scepticism about the formal preoccupations of the established

Civic Architects secured a sustainable future for the village of Gamlingay's formerly derelict community centre by adding spaces that can be rented out and and introducing green technologies.

Orkidstudio's £1K house was designed to be built by an unskilled female labour-force in Kenya.

avant-garde. This generation takes it as read that modernity and cultural continuity are reconcilable goals. For all the diversity of the featured practices, we therefore find that the forms and materials of pre-modern architecture represent common points of concern, while a widespread interest in the function of ornament – whether in the form of the parametrically-modeled designs of Acme and Serie or in Studio Weave and DK-CM's appeal to vernacular and pop traditions – is also much in evidence.

Above all, this is an architecture derived from the specific characteristics of local contexts. In a country as long-urbanised as the UK, these are commonly marked by the built contributions of many different time periods with the effect that the architect's task becomes one of forging a 'difficult whole' from heterogeneous parts. Those skills are foregrounded particularly clearly in the many projects featured here that have involved the adaptation of existing buildings. The frank juxtaposition of new and old – so frequently deployed by modern architects of earlier generations – has given way to a new paradigm: the synthesis of different periods of fabric to nuanced but ultimately unified effect.

A concern with developing work from each project's cultural specificities also informs a prevalent attitude to social engagement. Wary of the value of tokenistic community consultation, this generation is pioneering new ways of involving end-users in both the design and realisation of their work. In the case of Civic Architects, this interest extends to working with the voluntary sector to develop projects in response to local need. The remodeling of a formerly derelict community hall in the village of Gamlingay would certainly never have been achieved were it not for the architect's role in co-ordinating local community groups and securing multiple funding streams. The practice's involvement related as much to the design of the facility's business model as to its built form: tasks that were undertaken over the course of a decade in a sustained back and forth process. The creation of spaces that could provide a rental income ultimately proved central to ensuring the facility's longterm sustainability. So too was the building's environmental performance: photovoltaics provide all electricity, while solar water heaters and ground source heat pumps deal with heating and hot water.

Article 25 and Orkidstudio, define their mission in similarly multifaceted terms. Both are UK-based humanitarian organisations, focused on the provision of buildings for impoverished and disaster-hit communities across the third world. Frequently that goal requires the development of designs capable of being built by end-users. Orkidstudio's £1K house, for example, is a 60m² family home designed to be built using earthbags by unskilled women in Kenya. The project's value lies not only in its built legacy but also in the wider social empowerment that it has enabled. Delivered in some of the most challenging environments in the world, the work of these practices affirms architecture's continued capacity to foster civilisation and change lives.

Ellis Woodman is the Director of the Architecture Foundation

1 Nearly 400 architects declared insolvent in two years, Elizabeth Hopkirk, Building Design, 4 April 2013.

31/44 Architects' name refers to the country telephone codes for its dual locations in the Netherlands (Amsterdam) and the UK (London). The practice was established in 2010 by James Jeffries, Stephen Davies and William Burges, who also teaches an undergraduate studio at Kingston University.

Projects range in scale from strategic masterplanning through to residential work. These include refurbishing the conference facilities at The Barbican in London, a mixed-use retail and residential scheme in a historic South East of England town, and a masterplan for a retirement community overlooking the Mediterranean in Spain.

In 2015, the practice completed five buildings – four one-off houses in the UK and the Netherlands and a mixed-use retail and boutique hotel building on Redchurch Street, London. The latter is a refurbishment and two-storey extension of a 1960s light industrial building, and includes the addition of new charcoal concrete infill panels with exposed silver aggregate.

Opposite: 31/44 Architects works in both the
UK and the Netherlands. Amsterdam Row House,
a new-build house in Central Amsterdam, replaced
a dilapidated workers' cottage and contributes to
the eclectic quality of the street.

Below: House for a London Suburb, a redevelopment of an end of terrace workshop (bottom).
MDF model of a pre-cast concrete decorative panel
(top). The pattern is a reference to the traditional
tiling of Victorian hallways and paths.

A449 Set up in Edinburgh in 2010 by Matthew Johnson, A449 specialises in domestic new build, extensions and refurbishments.

The practice believes that domestic architecture has the potential to 'truly excite and delight'. Rosefield, an extension of a converted coach house in Edinburgh using charred timber cladding, won both an RIAS Award and Saltire Society Housing Design Award in 2015.

Orchard Neuk, a new build house in Gattonside in the Scottish Borders, was a finalist in the Edinburgh Architectural Association Awards 2014.

Other projects include three townhouses on an urban infill site in Edinburgh, an extension to a nursery school, and the extension and charred larch overcladding of Blakeburn Cottage, a 1950s property in the Scottish Borders.

A449 operated as a single-person practice until recently growing in tandem with increased turnover. As well as further multiple dwelling projects, the practice is interested in expanding into the affordable housing sector.

Opposite: Rosefield, a sympathetic extension and restoration of a former coach house in Portobello, Edinburgh, one of A449's many domestic projects.

Below: Orchard Neuk at Gattonside in the Scottish Borders replaced a bungalow with a much larger new build home. The upper storey is designed to appear as if floating above the glazed ground floor.

ACME was set up in London in 2007 by Friedrich Ludewig and Stefano Dal Piva, who originate from Germany and Italy respectively. ACME has since completed projects in 20 countries, opening additional offices in Sydney, Berlin and San Francisco.

The practice works across architecture, urban planning, interior and product design for private, corporate and public clients. Commissions vary in typology and scale from high-rise residential developments, banks, libraries and offices through to private villas and tree houses. ACME's Hunsett Mill in Norfolk won the RIBA Manser Medal for best house of the year in 2010.

ACME has also worked on inner city masterplans including the Smithfield Quarter in Birmingham, Eastgate Quarters in Leeds and Northgate in Chester.

Recent projects include a John Lewis store in Leeds, expansion of the Robina shopping mall in the Australian city of Gold Coast, and Watermark WestQuay, a mixed-use development in Southampton.

Opposite: Victoria Gate Arcade in Leeds. The building is designed as a two storey, twin arcade with a complex roofscape that continues the grand history of the city's 19th century arcades.

Below: Leeds' wool trade and its tradition of sculpted stone buildings inspired ACME's design for a John Lewis store in the Eastgate Quarter of the city (bottom). Prefabricated panels will be incorporated into the diagrid facade (top).

Previous spread: Hunsett Mill, Norfolk Broads.
An extension to the Grade II listed mill was conceived as a shadow of the existing house. The solid
laminated wood structure is clad in charred cedar
externally and exposed internally.

Below: Minories, London. Exterior view of residential building, part of a mixed-use regeneration of
a derelict site at Aldgate.

Below: ACME re-thought the traditional bank typology in its design (bottom) for the Sächsische AufbauBank (SAB) Forum/Saxony State Bank Headquarters in Leipzig, Germany. Inside (top) new public routes and spaces are conceived as clearings in a forest of supporting columns.

Adam Khan Architects

Established in 2006, Adam Khan Architects designs public buildings, social housing and private houses in both the UK and overseas.

In Denmark, a £22million regeneration of the Ellebo housing estate near Copenhagen, aims to create a sense of place and dignity. In London, the practice is designing social housing and community facilities for a number of progressive London boroughs including Hackney. Private residential projects include a pair of Arts and Crafts-influenced houses in Camden, London conceived in dialogue with each other and their neighbours.

The practice's competition-winning design for the Brockholes Visitor Centre in Lancashire created a cluster of buildings floating on a large pontoon and won both RIBA and Civic Trust Awards in 2012. It has since completed new facilities for Pensthorpe Natural Park in Norfolk.

The practice regards continuity and familiarity as essential as surprise and provocation, and describes itself as 'fascinated by the mysterious world of surfaces and things'.

Opposite and below: Brockholes Visitor Centre, near Preston. Designed on a pontoon, the nature reserve was created in a former gravel quarry.

Oak-clad visitor buildings are arranged around a series of sheltered courtyards (bottom right). Inside, the glulam structure is exposed (bottom left). View out over the lake (top).

Previous spread: Shared garden room at Ellebo, an
estate in Ballerup on the outskirts of Copenhagen.
Adam Khan Architects won a competition for the
sustainable refurbishment of the 1960s estate.

New Horizon Youth Centre, Kings Cross, London.
As part of a re-working of a centre for the home-
less, the project created the Barn performance
space (right), located on the first floor above
teaching, medical and wash facilities. The Barn's
oak-lined interior (left).

Play Barn, part of a new masterplan for Pensthorpe Natural Park in Norfolk. Timber cladding incorporates holes for potential future roosting boxes.

Adam Nathaniel Furman trained at the Architectural Association (AA) and works broadly across architecture, interiors, products, fine art and writing. He also teaches, and is director of the Saturated Space Research Cluster at the AA which explores the use of colour in architecture and urbanism.

As Designer in Residence at the Design Museum in London during 2013–14, Furman produced the Identity Parade collection of objects. Through the use of a fictional collector character, this considered how a designer might use rapid fabrication techniques as part of an investigation of their identity. In another residency after winning the Rome Prize for Architecture in 2014, Furman created The Roman Singularity, a multi-media piece based on Rome as a playground for the hyperactive architectural imagination.

Under the aegis of Madam Studio, which he co-founded with Marco Ginex, Furman completed a highly colourful refurbishment of a three bedroom maisonette within the listed Paragon terrace in Clifton, Bristol.

Opposite: Identity Parade, created as part of the Design Museum's 2013–14 Designers in Residence programme. Rapid fabrication techniques were used to explore identity and the roles of the designer and the collector.

Below: A tired maisonette within The Paragon, a Grade II* listed terrace in Clifton, Bristol, was extended and transformed into a vibrantly-coloured three bedroom apartment.

Overleaf: Memory Palace from The Roman Singularity, a multi-media exploration to create an imaginary alternative Rome for the 21st century. Designed as part of the Rome Prize for Architecture 2014–15.

Amin Taha set up his practice in 2005 followed in 2009 by Group Work, a companion organisation for collaborations with urban, graphic and furniture designers on competitions and built work.

Projects range in scale from masterplans through to renovations and furniture commissions. These include a proposal for La Herradura resort hotel in Spain that would create a sustainable, year round retreat community for 1200 inhabitants, and an ongoing infrastructure integration project for a new city quarter in Sofia, Bulgaria.

In London, the practice has won three RIBA Awards, the latest in 2014 for its refurbishment of a four storey, nineteenth century office building on Golden Lane. This combined the reinstatement of the original building fabric with judicious new additions, and also included the design of desks, plan chests and storage units.

Taha studied at De Montfort University, University of Edinburgh and UCL and has taught at Oxford Brookes, Edinburgh, Nottingham and Scott Sutherland schools of architecture.

Opposite and below: Hyde Park residential block, central London. Re-imagined 19th century bronze mesh elevation with mechanical openings (bottom). Bay study of type, perforation, density and variation (left). 1:1 prototype samples of solid bronze sill and corbel details (top).

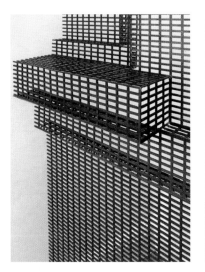

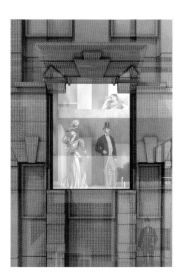

Model study for Sofia Metro Station, Bulgaria.
Amin Taha Architects won an international
design competition for the masterplan and
station design project.

Proposed refurbishment of an apartment in
the Barbican in the City of London (left). 1:1
prototype of brass screen support structure for
the apartment (right).

AOC aims to design generous architecture that is both beautiful and socially participative. Since setting up in east London in 2005 the practice has completed a diverse range of new buildings as well as exhibitions, public realm, interiors, products, temporary installations and neighbourhood masterplans.

The practice has particular experience developing new briefs for complex organisations, including the Reading Room for Wellcome Collection and the redevelopment of The National Archives in Kew.

AOC has delivered a number of educational buildings in London and the UK, including St Saviour's & St Olave's Secondary and the Spa School for young people with autism. For the University of Cambridge the practice has designed new postgraduate accommodation on a greenfield site in North West Cambridge. At Nunhead Green with the London Borough of Southwark, AOC has developed a brownfield site to provide new housing, an improved public space and The Green, a low-energy centre for a local community group.

Opposite and below: Nunhead Green, south east London. Sketch model (right) of the community centre with adjacent housing. The Green, community centre (left). The living room (bottom) in the centre of The Green connects all the meeting rooms and the rear garden beyond.

Overleaf: Spa Secondary School for pupils with autism in London's Southwark, one of several school projects completed by AOC.

Wellcome Reading Room, Euston, London.
A variety of table lengths, heights and seating
encourage visitors to interact with the artefacts
and each other as part of the room's transformation into a participative permanent gallery.

St Saviour's & St Olave's Secondary School for Girls in Southwark, London. Large scale lettering in precast concrete announces the school to the New Kent Road (top).

Detail of the precast concrete cornice and brickwork (bottom).

Archipelago Architects encompasses the collective work of James Payne and Nina
Lundvall as well as their collaborations with other disciplines and designers. Lundvall is
a project architect at Caruso St John Architects and Payne is a senior lecturer at the The
Cass School of Architecture, where the two run a teaching studio together. They established
Archipelago in 2007 in east London after previous competition collaborations.

Archipelago has designed housing and arts projects in both the UK and Sweden
for public and private clients. Built works include two domestic projects in south London,
one to create a garden room, the other a larger restructuring which involved the removal
and replacement of an extension. Archipelago also designed the 2007 exhibition Panic
Attack: Art in the Punk Years at the Barbican Art Gallery in London.

In Sweden, Archipelago has worked on a number of residential and summer houses
projects as well as accommodation for a sailing school in the Stockholm archipelago.

Opposite: Competition proposal for a mining and geological museum, Jøssingfjord, Norway (with Lorenzo de Chiffre, Vienna).

Below: Low-cost family house in Stockholm, one of Archipelago's many Swedish projects.

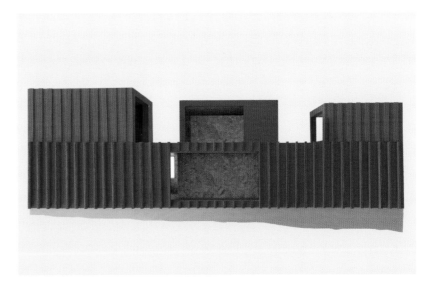

Architecture 00 Rather than following a traditional practice model with conventional disciplinary boundaries, Architecture 00 [zero zero] describes itself as 'a collaborative studio that is home to architects, social designers, economic & urban geographers, programmers, urban sociologists and psychologists, as well as others who struggle to define themselves through conventional roles'.

Architecture 00 pioneers open source design through its WikiHouse and OpenDesk initiatives and has designed the Impact Hub series of collaborative workspaces in London. 00 advocates participative processes, often co-designing, co-making, co-operating, and even co-owning projects with the end users.

The Foundry, a low-budget workplace for social justice and human rights organisations in London's Vauxhall won RIBA London's Building of the Year 2015. Further projects include Community Enterprise Centres, SOAR Works and Manor Works, which won RIBA Yorkshire Building of the Year in 2014 and 2013 respectively and the refurbishment of Greenpeace UK's headquarters.

Practice research includes A Right to Build, which investigates self-provided housing, and Compendium for the Civic Economy.

Opposite and below: iCity Colosseum Olympic Car Park. Invited ideas competition entry that proposed turning a piece of Olympic infrastructure into a platform for urban events.

Overleaf: The Foundry, Vauxhall, south London. A deep, concrete-framed front extension was added as part of the former factory's conversion into a social justice hub.

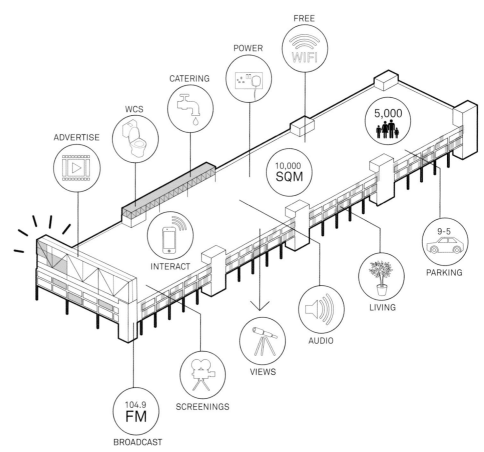

The WikiHouse open source construction system utilises digital manufacturing to enable anyone to design, print and assemble customised, low energy houses.

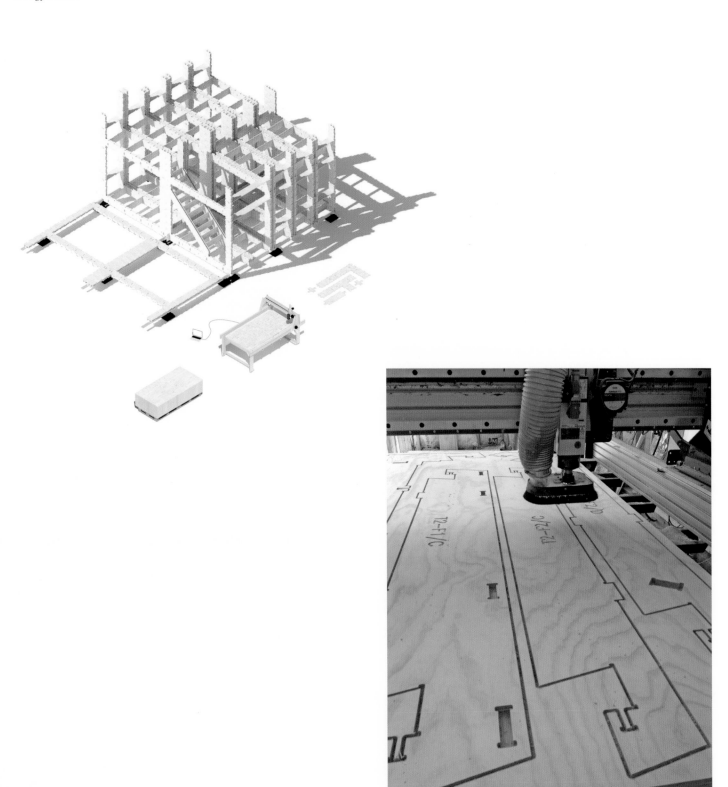

Construction of Farmhouse, Rugby (top) and
A-Barn, West Scotland (bottom), both designed
and built using the WikiHouse system.

Article 25 designs, builds and manages projects in vulnerable and disaster-hit communities worldwide.

Set up by Maxwell Hutchinson after the 2004 earthquake and tsunami, the architectural aid charity is named after the 25th article of the Universal Declaration of Human Rights – the right to adequate living standards.

The charity works widely in Africa, Asia and South America building schools, healthcare buildings and housing. It has extensive experience designing and delivering earthquake-resistant buildings in Pakistan, Afghanistan and in Nepal, where it is developing schools and housing. Article 25 has been active in Haiti since the 2010 earthquake. Projects include the design of a new primary school in Pétionville in collaboration with Outreach International.

All projects seek to use local materials and involve local communities in the building process. Completed buildings include a training centre for former child soldiers in northern Uganda, a children's home in Ghana, and post-war school reconstruction in the Democratic Republic of Congo.

Opposite: Bethel Secondary School, Gourcy, Burkina Faso. Built using locally sourced materials such as laterite stone, the school design provides protection from the extremely hot climate.

Below: Gola Forest Conservation Area Headquarters, Sierra Leone. Render (top) and photograph (bottom right) of the project, built in collaboration with local villagers (bottom left).

Asif Khan established his London-based architecture office in 2007 after studying at
The Bartlett and the Architectural Association, where he spent a year researching refugee
housing on the Thai-Burma border.

Projects range from exhibitions and installations to cultural buildings and masterplans. He has had particular success with temporary pavilions, winning an Architecture
Foundation competition to design Coca-Cola's London 2012 Olympic Park pavilion. His
Beatbox design contained embedded sounds of sports that were triggered as visitors moved
through the pavilion. At the Sochi 2014 Winter Olympics, Khan's MegaFaces pavilion for
telecoms network MegaFon created the faces of visitors in its 8metres-high kinetic facade.

Permanent buildings include the West Beach Café in Littlehampton. He was shortlisted
out of more than 1700 entries for the Guggenheim Helsinki competition.

In 2015, Khan was included in the Debrett's 500 list of top influencers and achievers
in British society. He is a trustee at the Design Museum.

Opposite and below: Guggenheim Museum Helsinki competition (finalist). A central wide staircase (left) was proposed to help visitors wayfind intuitively through the museum.

The translucent textured form (below) uses a 'smart' double-wall glass skin to encompass timber galleries within.

Coca-Cola Beatbox at the London 2012 Olympic Games. Innovative sound technology was embedded within ETFE cushions to create a piece of architecture that visitors could play like a musical instrument.

MegaFaces pavilion, conceived for the Sochi
Winter Olympic and Paralympic Games in 2014
(left). The kinetic facade used more than 11,000
actuators to create the portraits of visitors to
the building in three dimensions. One thousand
pin prototype, Shenzhen (right).

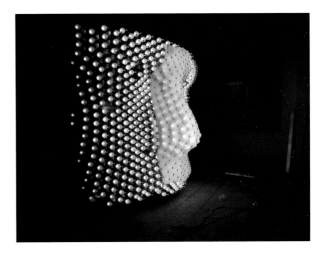

Assemble is a multi-disciplinary collective of 14 members working across architecture, design and art.

Based in London, they began working together in 2010 on the Cineroleum, a self-initiated project that transformed an abandoned petrol station on Clerkenwell Road, central London into a cinema.

Assemble describes itself as 'committed to both the practice of making things and the practice of making things happen'. It seeks to actively engage the public as participant and collaborator in its work, which includes community playgrounds, affordable workspace, arts venues and improvements to public space. Often improvised and temporary, the work is characterised by an emphasis on the process of construction, and the activities of the spaces created, as well as the completed building form.

In 2015, Assemble won the Turner Prize for its Granby Four Streets project in Toxteth, a collaboration with locals to refurbish housing, public space and provide new work and enterprise opportunities.

Opposite and below: Granby Four Streets, a community-led initiative to refurbish housing and public space and create enterprise opportunities in a cluster of terraced streets in Toxteth, Liverpool. Model (left). Isometric (bottom). Improved streetscape (right). Ducie Street greenhouse (top).

Overleaf: The Cineroleum, a self-initiated project that transformed a petrol station on London's Clerkenwell Road into a cinema using cheap industrial, reclaimed and donated materials.

Yardhouse, an affordable workspace in Stratford, east London, was designed and built by Assemble for the London Legacy Development Corporation. Timber frame (top). Completed interior (left). Handmade concrete tile cladding (bottom).

Assemble is creating a public art gallery for Goldsmiths University in south London within a former Victorian bathhouse (left). Interventions include a new clerestory gallery (right).

AY Architects works in the education, residential, community and public realm sectors. The practice was established in 2006 by Yeoryia Manolopoulou and Anthony Boulanger, who teach at The Bartlett School of Architecture and University of Westminster respectively.

The practice is particularly concerned with the social purpose of architecture, generating projects itself to bring about incremental urban change. One of these self-instigated projects, the Montpelier Community Nursery, won a 2013 RIBA National Award and the 2013 Stephen Lawrence Prize for the best building in the UK with a construction budget of under £1 million.

AY Architects' highest profile project has been the festive installation House of Flags for the Greater London Authority. Constructed from 206 interlocking flag panels, this was erected on Parliament Square to celebrate the 2012 Olympic and Paralympic Games. Another installation, City Boardwalks, proposed a pedestrian walkway and potted plant landscape as a temporary enhancement of the 122 Leadenhall site. Further projects include upcoming extensions to Camden School for Girls.

Opposite and below: Montpelier Community Nursery, Kentish Town, London.

After a land swap, the new building gives more space and a bench to the public gardens (left). Entrance (right). Continuity between interior play area and outdoor landscape (below).

House of Flags, Parliament Square, London.
Built from 206 interconnecting flag panels, the
installation (top) references Charles and Ray
Eames' House of Cards toy. Panel detail (bottom).

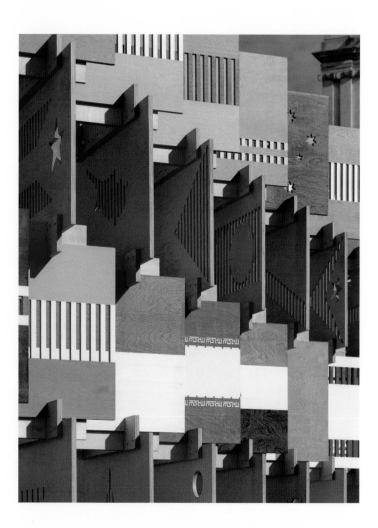

Planted landscape and demountable boardwalks, 122 Leadenhall, London. The proposal was a finalist in a 2009 competition for the temporary enhancement of stalled construction sites in the City of London.

Baxendale Design Co is led by architect and artist Lee Ivett, a design tutor and lecturer at Glasgow School of Art. The multi-disciplinary design practice has a focus on ethical arts, installation and community projects, working in collaboration with artists, makers, dancers, choreographers, growers, academics and musicians.

Baxendale works with communities and individuals with the aim of improving their experience of life through design interventions that engage and inspire. The practice takes a hands-on approach to creating the conditions for participation from conception to completion. The intention is to deliver a design with longevity that is aspirational, affordable and valued.

Baxendale has worked within the public realm, the theatre, the gallery and the home in locations as diverse as Los Angeles, Preston, and Nuremburg. Glasgow interventions include Woodlands Community Garden, a growing space and social hub delivered using volunteer community labour, and De Anderen, a creative space constructed using reclaimed timber, packaging crates and pallets.

Opposite: Sanctuary, a pavilion of reflective space within the ruins of Caledonia Road Church, Glasgow, constructed from more than 600 pieces of bamboo.

Below: Project MOTO, developed as part of BIO50 24th Biennial of Design Ljubljana, Slovenia in response to underused space on post-war housing estates. Following concept development (bottom), the outcome (top) is an object for adaptation, development and enhancement by the community.

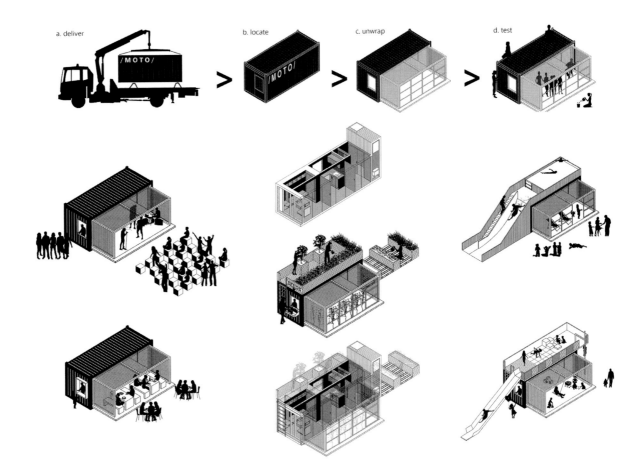

Bell Phillips Tim Bell and Hari Phillips set up their practice after winning a RIBA competition in 2005 to regenerate the Brooks Road Estate in Plaistow, Newham.

Bell Phillips's core work is affordable housing. The practice has assisted more than half of the London boroughs on housing delivery programmes with the aim of establishing new quality standards in this sector. Projects include a prototype single storey housetype for people over 60 years for the Royal Borough of Greenwich.

At Heron Court in Thamesmead, the practice completed an 18-unit canalside development using untreated timber, galvanized steel and brick. It is working on the relocation of the Grade II listed Gasholder No.8 at King's Cross to a new public space alongside Regent's Canal.

At Skinners' School in Tunbridge Wells, Bell Phillips has planning consent for a three storey, arts and literature building designed with angled brick details and repetitive bays in response to the adjacent Victorian school buildings.

Opposite and below: Heron Court, an 18-unit
affordable housing development in Thamesmead,
south east London. Elevations are articulated
by a series of timber and galvanised steel fins.

Gasholder No.8, King's Cross Central, London.
Bell Phillips worked with Argent on a methodology
for the dismantling, refurbishment and re-erec-
tion of the Victorian structure as part of new
public realm elsewhere on the site.

Arts & Literature building, The Skinners' School, Tunbridge Wells, Kent. Proposed new building (top).

Elevation, showing the three storey intervention in context between two Victorian buildings (bottom).

Carl Trenfield's practice is based in Canterbury, a city where he studied architecture and later – while at Keith Williams Architects – worked on the design of the Marlowe Theatre.

The practice works closely with makers and builders to explore both traditional and contemporary notions of craft and fabrication. Great emphasis is placed on drawing, modeling and prototyping.

Projects include a study for an affordable, floating, housing community for water-based housing specialist Ecofloat, with whom the practice has a close collaborative relationship.

The practice has completed a number of residential projects including the renovation of a Victorian house in Blackheath, where it worked closely with a craftsman on fixed and loose furniture, and the refurbishment of several Span properties on the nearby Cator Estate. In Canterbury, completed projects include the renovation of the Grade II listed C16 Ivy Cottage including the sensitive integration of a new galley kitchen and storage device.

Opposite: Prefabricated, double-skinned stair with integrated copper rods, designed as part of a renovation and remodeling of a split level Victorian apartment in Snaresbrook, east London.

Below: The renovation of a Victorian residence on Dartmouth Row, south London, features bespoke joinery including hand made steps (top) and laser-etched and hand-turned door furniture (bottom left). View to study from living area (bottom right).

Carl Turner Architects

Established in 2006, Carl Turner Architects (CTA) has established a reputation for high impact, low cost architecture.

Housing is a particular focus. CTA won the Manser Medal in 2013 for Slip House, a Code for Sustainable Homes Level 5 standard house in Brixton clad in translucent glass. The practice was joint winner of the RIBA's Housing in the Private Rental Market ideas competition in 2013.

CTA's work is informed by physically testing and developing ideas through the process of construction, with the practice often acting as its own contractor. It aims to employ inclusive processes that enable the individual or stakeholder group.

CTA is interested in place-making and the creation of active rather than passive public space. It has explored this on projects such as Pop Brixton, a community campus for start-ups and small businesses, and Peckham Library Square, where CTA is working on improvements with a co-design community engagement programme.

Opposite: Slip House, Brixton, south London.
A prototype for adaptable terrace housing,
the house won the Manser Medal in 2013.

Below: Pop Brixton, Brixton, south London.
Entrance (top) of Pop Brixton, a community
campus for startups, small businesses and
community groups. Polytunnel (bottom),
part of the community gardening component,
at the campus opening.

Carmody Groarke
Established in London by Kevin Carmody and Andrew Groarke in 2006, Carmody Groarke works widely across the private, commercial and public sectors.

The practice has had particular success with cultural projects, designing a temporary White Cube gallery at Glyndebourne and a visitor pavilion at Waddesdon Manor for the Rothschild Foundation, both in 2015. It won a competition for the Windermere Jetty Museum in Cumbria and is designing Dorset County Museum's new Collections Discovery Centre, as well as exhibitions for several leading cultural institutions.

Its work in other sectors includes Carmody Groarke's highest profile project, the 7 July Memorial in London's Hyde Park, which used cast steel pillars to represent the 52 lives lost. In 2014 it completed Maggie's Merseyside at Clatterbridge, the cancer support organisation's first temporary centre.

The practice won a RIBA London Small Project Award for The Filling Station, a conversion of a derelict petrol station in King's Cross into a public events space and restaurant.

Opposite and below: Windermere Jetty Museum will house the museum's boat collection at Lake Windermere in the Lake District National Park.

Site drawing (below), renders (left and top right) and model (middle right) show facilities arranged to give an active lake edge. Section (bottom) showing central wet dock.

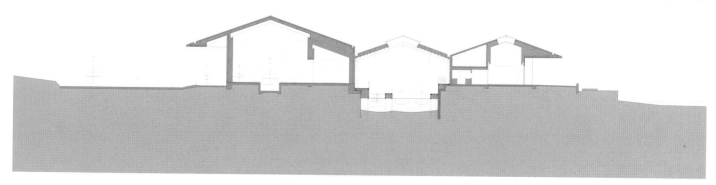

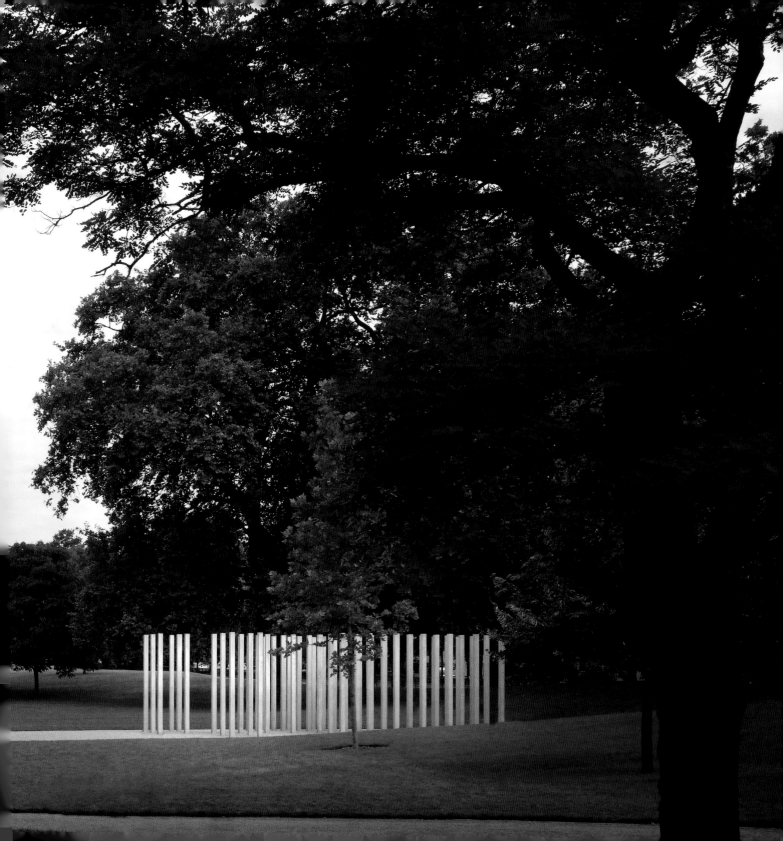

Previous spread: 7 July Memorial, Hyde Park, London. Stainless steel pillars in four interlinked clusters represent each of the 52 lives lost.

Below: Black Forest Visitor Centre, Germany. Views of the model and, below right, section.

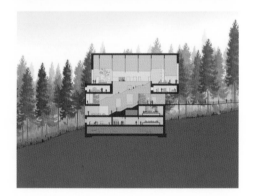

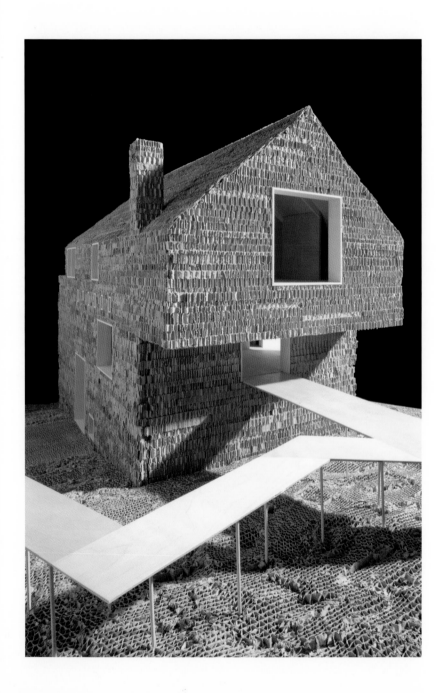

Rectory Farm, Hounslow, west London. Proposal to create a one kilometre long landscaped public park. Render (top); Site drawing (bottom).

CarverHaggard was set up in 2010 by Josh Carver and William Haggard, who studied together at Cambridge University and previously held senior roles at Adjaye Associates and DSDHA. Since 2011, they have taught together at the Cass School of Architecture in East London.

The Brixton-based practice works to create public spaces and public benefit. Projects range from conventional architectural and design work to technical research and economic strategy. Clients include universities in Germany, private developers in South-East Asia, and community groups in London.

In Singapore, CarverHaggard designed an open-air gallery inspired by the local 'Black and White' house type which combines vernacular typologies and half-timbered decoration. The practice created another gallery in an industrial district in Kuala Lumpur, combining steel-framed exhibition sheds with a sheltered central garden.

CarverHaggard's research explores contemporary vernacular and informal inhabitation of public spaces in London and Asia, including the utilisation of vacant urban sites by car washes.

Opposite and below: Black & White Gallery,
Singapore. The open air gallery draws on Malayan
vernacular and British half-timbered decoration.
View of external gallery (left). Gallery and garden
seen from the café (right).

Industrial Estate Gallery, Kuala Lumpur, Malaysia. Entrance (left).

View of main gallery from garden (right). Exhibition spaces are accommodated in a series of steel-framed sheds with highly glazed ground levels.

Modern Follies, Academy of Visual Arts in Leipzig, Germany. Collaboration with students at the Academy to animate an underused courtyard using a pavilion and mobile stair (bottom left).

Pavilion detail (top). The mobile stair acts as an auditorium for debates and performances (bottom right).

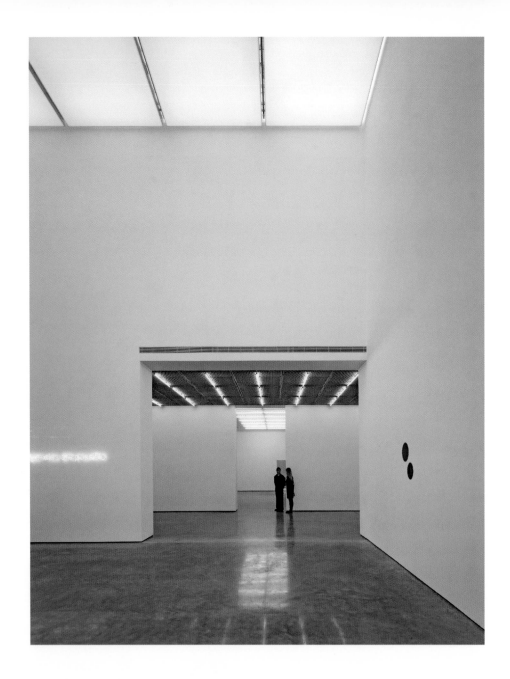

Casper Mueller Kneer Architects was established in 2010 by Mueller Kneer Associates in London and Büro Jens Casper in Berlin.

The practice has particular expertise in projects for the arts, fashion and culture. Among its London projects are the conversion of a former warehouse into the White Cube Bermondsey gallery and the design of The Institute of Sexology, a temporary exhibition at the Wellcome Trust in Euston.

Casper Mueller Kneer has completed several commissions for fashion house Céline – including three catwalk shows and their flagship store in London's Mount Street. Completed in 2014, this incorporates a parquet floor of more than 5000 pieces of marble.

Proposed London projects include the design of the new Ministry of Sound headquarters and club in Borough and a scheme for 32 housing units in Ilford. The practice also works extensively internationally with current work in Hong Kong, Korea, Japan, Egypt and Germany as well as the UK.

Opposite: White Cube Bermondsey, London. The gallery's third and largest venue in London was created in a 1970s former warehouse. Accommodation includes public and private galleries, an auditorium, bookshop, archive, art storage and offices.

Below: Ministry of Sound, Borough, London. Interior (top) and exterior (bottom) perspectives of relocation proposal. The design focuses on connectivity and separation to support the complex activities of the client including club, performance, exhibition, studios, restaurant and offices.

Cassion Castle Architects was established in 2006. Led by Cassion Castle, the North London practice has worked for private and commercial clients across the residential, leisure and education sectors. Unusually, it works as both architect and contractor for many of its projects.

The practice aims to create designs that represent the clients and context as much as itself. Completed projects include the Long Sutton Studio, a multi-purpose outbuilding for a furniture designer in Hampshire, designed to celebrate timber in its many forms. In Dalston, the practice has converted a former mews coach house into a photographer's studio and archive.

Oak Lane House, a new build family home in Suffolk, draws on local vernacular with a knapped flint ground floor set beneath a black timber upper storey. Brick Studio, a workspace for a product designer in East London, proposes a brick elevation with intermittent spacing, creating a scattered pattern to give a surprising effect when lit from within.

Opposite: Brick Studio, east London. This project proposes an anonymous exterior that merges seamlessly with adjacent buildings in response to the rugged street environment. Intermittent gaps in the brickwork create a scattered pattern.

Below: Coast House on the South Coast of England. This transformation of an existing house creates a fortress-like street elevation (bottom) with more extensive windows set back from the elevation overlooking the beach (left, right).

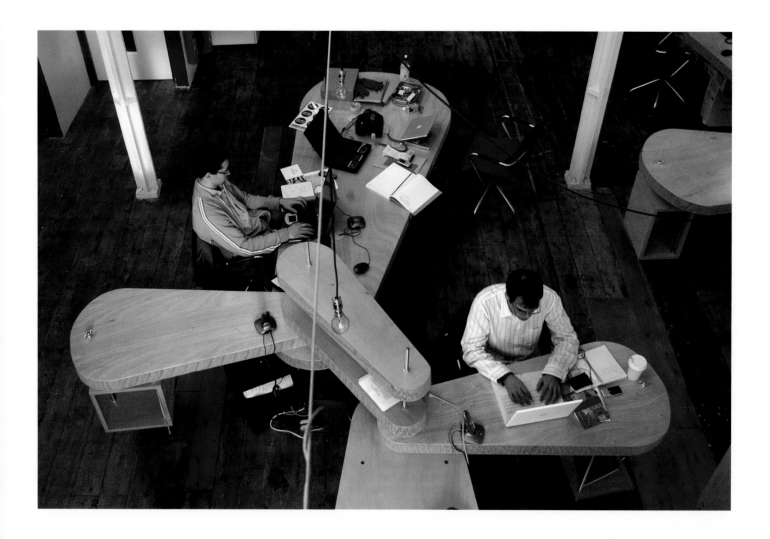

Citizens Design Bureau is a co-operative practice of architects and product designers established by Katy Marks in 2012.

Marks previously co-founded the co-working social enterprise ImpactHub before working for Haworth Tompkins, where she was project architect for the National Theatre Studios and Young Vic Theatre in London, and the Everyman Theatre in Liverpool.

Citizens Design Bureau works in the arts, community, workspace, and private residential sectors. Theatre projects include interior furniture, fittings and signage for the Everyman, the refurbishment of the Royal Court Theatre bar in London's Sloane Square (in collaboration with Lyndon Goode Architects) and the interior of the Sondheim Theatre for Sir Cameron Mackintosh in London's West End. Other work ranges from workshops and studios to a children's nursery, a live music venue, and a private house for film director Stephen Daldry.

In 2015, Marks was shortlisted for the Architects' Journal's Emerging Woman Architect of the Year Award.

Opposite: ImpactHub Islington, London. Plywood and cardboard furniture at the co-working social enterprise co-founded by Citizens Design Bureau's Katy Marks.

Below: Sondheim Theatre, central London. The project extensively re-models an existing London West End theatre for Sir Cameron Mackintosh. Watercolour (top) of the theatre interior. Plasterwork detail (bottom) on a full-scale model of a section of the theatre's balcony.

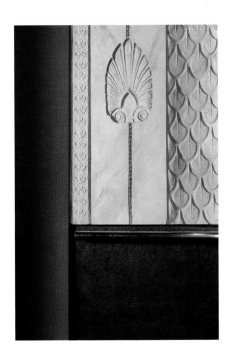

Civic's practice focuses on community-led architecture and public art. Based in London and Edinburgh, Civic was established by Dan Jones and Andrew Siddall in 2006 and is driven by an advocacy of user engagement with art and architecture. Civic works collaboratively with voluntary and community organisations using a 'demand-led' process that aims to enable client groups to lead the design process through their position as lay people. By working with those who stand to gain directly from getting involved, Civic hopes its projects benefit from a solid foundation of community engagement.

Key projects include Gamlingay Eco Hub, a re-purposed community centre in South Cambridgeshire that in 2012 was the first community centre in the country to incorporate three different passive technologies without fossil fuel backup. Recent work includes the roof-level refurbishment and extension of the Royals Youth Centre in Rainham, which includes a prominent new enterprise space cantilevered over the entrance.

Opposite: Rainham Royals Youth Centre in east London. The cantilevering Enterprise Space sits atop the existing refurbished building.

Below: Gamlingay Eco-Hub in south Cambridgeshire. View towards the entrance (top) showing the extension wrapping around the existing community centre. The flexible-use foyer (bottom) contains the reception and a foldaway library.

Coffey Architects
Set up in 2005, Coffey Architects specialises in residential, public and commercial work.

Founder Phil Coffey describes the practice's approach as driven by both an empathy for the users of the places it creates and by a desire to improve the physical, social and environmental context of each site.

Coffey Architects has designed several projects for major cultural institutions including the British Film Institute's Reuben Library, created out of a former black box gallery using a series of bronze mesh curtains. The practice has completed a large number of one-off new build houses and extensions and won the RIBA Stephen Lawrence Prize in 2011 for Book Box, a library extension and music room at St Patrick's School in north London.

Prior to setting up his own practice, Coffey worked for Ian Ritchie Architects on arts projects such as the Plymouth Theatre Royal production centre and the Spire of Dublin.

Opposite: British Film Institute Reuben Library, London. Bronze mesh curtains form a partial enclosure to the study spaces, created in a former black box gallery.

Below: Oaks Prague, Bohemia, Czech Republic. Coffey is one of ten practices working on the high end residential and leisure development. Cast concrete concept model (top). View towards the village square (bottom).

Folded House, Islington, north London. Extension of a five bedroom house. View from the garden, (top).

Main living space (bottom).

The Cloister, a 40,000m² headquarters
completed in Qingdao, China for Qingdao
Iron and Steel Company.

Coombs Jones

Based in Cardiff, Coombs Jones combines design, research, making and teaching with the aim of creating simple, well-crafted places.

The practice was founded in 2011 by architects Matthew Jones and Steve Coombs. Both founders teach as well as undertaking PhD research, on, respectively, the role of design in market towns and innovative design uses for Welsh timber.

Work ranges from furniture and installations to urban scale studies and settlement planning. Coombs Jones makes prototypes and experiments with materials as part of its research-based design process.

Housing sector work includes research on delivering high quality homes in Swansea for the Design Commission for Wales, as well as individual projects such as live-work housing in Raven Lane, Ludlow. In 2012, Coombs Jones won an open competition for an architecture pavilion at the Welsh National Eisteddfod with a design based on an abstraction of a Welsh landscape.

Opposite: Raven Lane live-work, Ludlow. Large scale physical model exploring inhabitation of a live-work courtyard home in the historic core of the Shropshire market town.

This page: Eisteddfod Architecture Pavilion 2012. Plan, section & exploded axonometric (right) of the pavilion, which represented aspects of the Welsh landscape. Internal view (left) of The Vessel performance space, an abstraction of the Welsh cave.

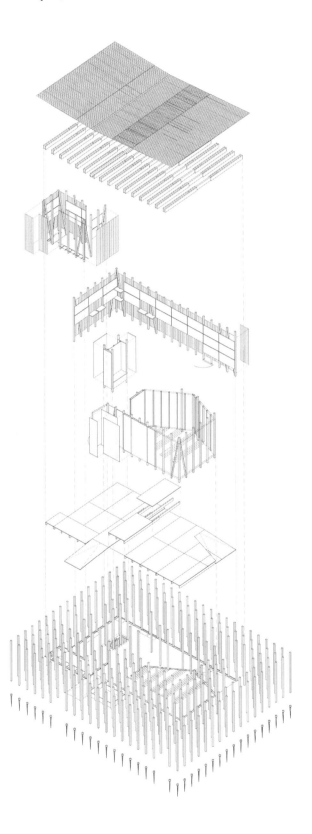

Dallas Pierce Quintero

Jonathan Dallas, David Pierce and Juliet Quintero set up in practice in 2009 after winning the Architecture Foundation's Amelia Street public realm competition.

Dallas Pierce Quintero (DPQ)'s work encompasses architecture, public art, cultural strategies, placemaking and engagement activities. A number of its projects deal with creative solutions for London's infill sites.

For the Royal Academy of Arts, DPQ was one of four practices chosen to put forward solutions to the housing crisis as part of the Future of Housing exhibition. DPQ's proposed nine alternative approaches such as microflats and the utilisation of left-over urban spaces. Its Courtyard House project, a new-build 95sqm infill house built on the site of a former builder's yard, won a London Regional Award and Small Project Award at the 2015 RIBA Awards.

DPQ's Towards Stillness installation at Leicester Cathedral used varying qualities of steel to convey the timeline between King Richard III's death and the discovery of his remains.

Opposite and below: Towards Stillness, Leicester Cathedral, Leicester. Sculpture celebrating the discovery of the remains of King Richard III. View showing its relationship to Leicester Cathedral (left). Silhouettes cut from steel panels (right) reveal the last journey of King Richard III.

Below and opposite: Courtyard House, east London. Built on an infill site, this two bedroom house won RIBA London Best Small Project in 2015. View towards kitchen and entrance.

Open plan living and dining spaces.

Rear external courtyard with black cement cladding and brickwork.

David Kohn Architects Established in London by David Kohn, DKA works internationally on arts, education, residential and urban design projects.

DKA describes itself as committed to the social relevance of architecture, craftsmanship in construction and the impact of projects on their wider surroundings.

It specializes in spaces for art, having designed five galleries in London and – in collaboration with artist Fiona Banner – creating A Room for London, an installation in the form of a boat on the roof of the Queen Elizabeth Hall on London's South Bank. The practice is also refurbishing the Institute of Contemporary Arts in London.

Residential projects include Carrer Avinyó, a refurbished Barcelona apartment which won World Interior of the Year in 2013. Stable Acre, a holiday home in rural Norfolk, won a RIBA Regional Award in 2012.

On a larger scale, DKA won a competition in 2015 to design 5000sqm quadrangle development of student facilities for New College, Oxford.

Opposite and below: A Room for London, a one-room installation perched on top of the Queen Elizabeth Hall at London's South Bank Centre (left, middle). View through the kitchen to the bedroom (bottom). Porthole window detail (right).

Overleaf: Carrer Avinyó, a *piano nobile* apartment in the Gothic Quarter of Barcelona, Spain, refurbished as a holiday home for two brothers.

New College, Oxford. Competition-winning
design for a new quad. Pictured: New entrance
on Mansfield Road.

Heterotopia, a network of park arts spaces
in the East Thames corridor (top). Model showing
spaces for artists to work in (bottom).

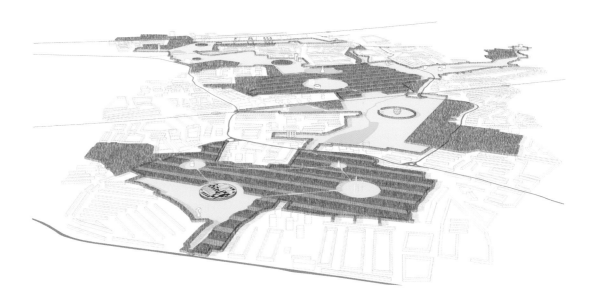

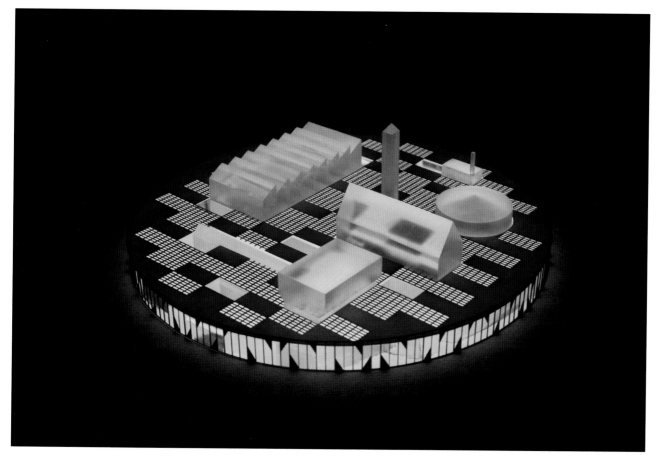

Delvendahl Martin
Nikolai Delvendahl and Eric Martin describe themselves as working from London with an international outlook. Both studied overseas and worked for Adjaye Associates and Allies and Morrison respectively before establishing their practice in 2009.

Delvendahl Martin avoids specialisation and instead works on diverse projects for private individuals, artists and public organisations.

The practice created a new headquarters and offices for Bow Arts Trust in east London in 2014 and collaborated with artist Carsten Höller on his Decision exhibition at the Hayward Gallery on London South Bank in 2015.

Commercial workspaces include the refurbishment and extension of offices in Hammersmith and a scheme to refurbish the former Crédit Lyonnais headquarters building at 30 Cannon Street in London.

Among the practice's completed residential projects are the conversion of two semi-detached houses in Oxford into one family home, and ZB House, a reworking and extension of a Victorian terrace house in north London.

Opposite: Rear view of Semi-Detached, Oxford. This project converted two semi-detached Victorian houses into one family home.

Below: New headquarters and office space for Bow Arts, an arts educational charity east London. Courtyard and canopy (top). Main approach (bottom).

Denizen Works was set up in London in 2011 by Murray Kerr, who formerly led the Netherlands studio of BDP.

Work ranges across many different types, locations and scales but is always driven, according to the practice, by an understanding of place and an emphasis on collaboration.

Private houses are a key strand of work. Denizen Works won the Stephen Lawrence Prize in 2014 for House No.7, built on the Isle of Tiree in the Inner Hebrides and conceived as a mix of traditional black house and agricultural steadings. On the island of Åland in Finland, the practice designed and built a temporary, 6sqm domestic sauna on runners so that it could be towed down to the water for an icy plunge.

Other diverse projects include a community building for a park in London, a master-plan for a rural airport and proposals for a floating cinema in Venice.

Opposite: Denizen Sauna, Åland, Finland. In response to planning restrictions, the 6m² mobile sauna was built on runners so that it can be towed down to the shore during winter months to allow users to plunge into the icy waters.

Below: House No. 7, Isle of Tiree, Scotland. Restored blackhouse with agricultural additions (top). The main gathering space (bottom).

DK-CM is an East London-based architecture and research studio founded by David Knight and Cristina Monteiro. Work ranges in scale from furniture through to masterplanning, urbanism and policy.

In Barkingside in east London, DK-CM designed a new town square and park in 2012–15, with the aim of creating a new civic language in dialogue with the adjacent 1960s library and swimming pool designed by Frederick Gibberd.

In 2011 the practice designed Folk in a Box, the world's smallest performance space accommodating an audience of one. The box's installations include Common Ground, the 13th International Architecture Exhibition of the Venice Biennale.

Other projects include public space interventions in Southall (2012–2015), and a rooftop space for the Paul Hamlyn Foundation in King's Cross (2012–14).

DK-CM has a particular interest in the processes by which places change, producing self-initiated projects such as Building Rights, an online repository of planning knowledge for the public.

Opposite and below: Barkingside Town Square, a new civic and commercial space utilising spaces around 1960s civic buildings designed by Frederick Gibberd. Part of the Better Barkingside initiative.

Below Right: Detail of Virginia Gardens, a new high street park created behind Fullwell Cross Leisure Centre as part of the Better Barkingside initiative.

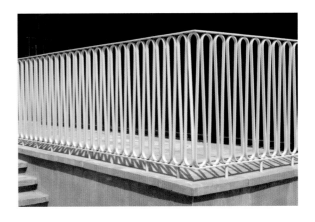

New square at Southall Green in the centre of old
Southall (bottom), one of several DK-CM-designed
public realm projects in the area. Isometric
(top). The square is a collaboration with Urban
Movement and Project Centre.

Folk in a Box, the world's smallest performance venue (top). The one audience member box appeared at the Venice Biennale, and has since toured the UK (bottom).

Dominic McKenzie set up his practice in 2011. He was previously a director at Alison Brooks Architects (ABA), where he was project architect for the ABA part of Accordia, the Stirling Prize-winning housing development in Cambridge.

Dominic McKenzie Architects has completed a variety of residential extension and new build projects most notably Eidolon House on Swains Lane next to Highgate Cemetery in north London. Clad in mirror-polished stainless steel to reflect the mature trees opposite, the house won the one-off house category of the Sunday Times British Homes Awards in 2014.

At Bower House, a Grade II listed house in Islington, the practice's renovation and extension included the addition of 5metre high French doors to completely open up the house to the garden. The practice has secured planning permission for a one-bedroom plus one-office house on a brownfield site in Dalston, east London featuring a geometric flower-patterned facade inspired by that of a nearby listed church.

Opposite: Eidolon House in Highgate, believed to be the first mirror-clad house in London. View down Swains Lane showing trees reflected in the mirror-polished stainless steel.

Below: Rendering of a new build house proposed for Dalston, east London. The patterned cladding is inspired by the facade of a nearby church.

Duggan Morris Architects has enjoyed considerable growth and success since its foundation in 2005. Led by Mary Duggan and Joe Morris, the practice has won multiple awards including the Manser Medal in 2011 for its renovation of a 1960s Brutalist building in Highgate, north London, and the Stephen Lawrence Prize in 2012 for the King's Grove new build house in south London. Ortus, the home of Maudsley Learning in Camberwell, won a RIBA London and RIBA National Award.

Duggan Morris chooses not to specialise and instead works across a broad range of typologies, locations and sectors including housing, workplace, residential and education.

Notable recent work includes a 45-unit housing development at Brentford Lock West, a pool house with a sculptural pitched roof at Alfriston School in Buckinghamshire, and a major office development at London's King's Cross. Designed for Argent, the latter provides 14,000 sqm of office accommodation plus an independent three-screen cinema.

Opposite and below: Ortus Maudsley Learning Centre, Camberwell, south London. Pre-cast concrete fins articulate the elevation of this mental health learning facility (left, right). Learning space interior (below left). Generous circulation (below right).

Overleaf: Swimming Pool at Alfriston School, a special needs girls school in Buckinghamshire. The form evokes the surrounding vernacular of Arts and Crafts buildings using a prefabricated, cross laminated timber frame.

Brentford Lock West housing. Designed for ISIS Waterside Regeneration, the roof form takes cues from nearby housing schemes as well as adjacent agricultural and industrial sheds.

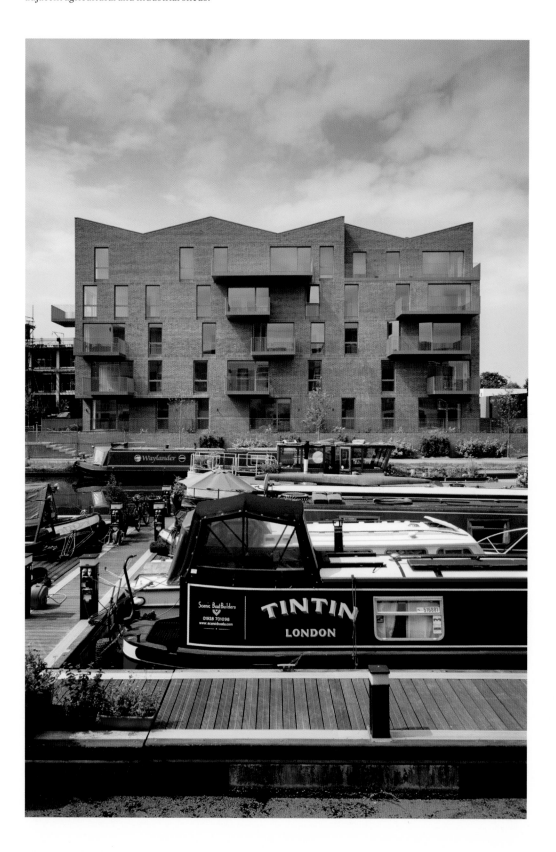

King's Cross R7, London. Study model for mixed-
use office building. The proposed building will
face the Grade II-Listed Granary Building and
Transit Sheds as well as the Midlands Goods Shed.

Dyvik Kahlen Architects is a London-based office run by Christopher Dyvik and Max Kahlen. Established in 2010, the practice works mainly in London, Holland and Germany.

In 2013, Dyvik Kahlen completed London's Smallest House, a 14.1m² house arranged over three levels in Islington, north London. This was pre-fabricated in Holland and installed on site within eight days. Other London projects include the exhibition design of Magnificent Obsessions at the Barbican Art Gallery; a low-cost artist studio underneath a viaduct in Muswell Hill; refurbishment of the Walther König Bookshop at Whitechapel Art Gallery; and a warehouse apartment for an artist and his family in Kilburn.

In Germany, Dyvik Kahlen is working on two new apartment buildings and a villa in Aachen, a penthouse in Cologne, and a temporary restaurant next to the Rhine. In Holland, projects include a park with zero-energy industrial units and a new service building and public space for t'Raboes harbour in Eemnes.

Opposite and below: Small House, Islington,
London. Axonometric (centre) of the 14.1m²
house, created on the site of a former flower shop.
Exterior view from street (left) towards the kitchen,
showing steps leading to the bedroom (right).

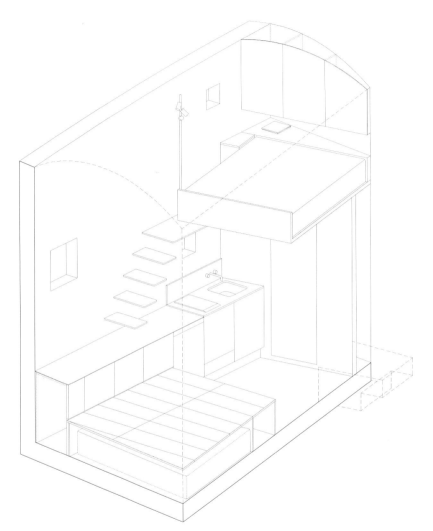

Twin Arch Studio, London. The new build
artist studios were created beneath a viaduct.
View of the rear facade through the viaduct
(left). Inside the studio (right).

Collage of facade for Villa P, Aachen, Germany. The building comprises two apartments with private rooms on the ground floor, large living rooms on the upper floor and a roof garden.

Emulsion is led by Yen-Yen Teh and Michael Deeley, who met while studying architecture at the University of Cambridge.

Clients range from new business start-ups to established corporate brands and public bodies. Projects include a reception and gallery for the British Council, a flagship Chelsea store for jeweler Monica Vinader, several outlets for the Apostrophe café chain and office design for advertising agency Karmarama. The practice recently secured planning permission for three new residential units clad in brick, charred timber and mesh on a site on Albany Road opposite Burgess Park in south London.

Outside the UK, Emulsion has undertaken private residential and commercial retail work in Europe, the Caribbean and the Far East.

With a focus on materiality, precise detailing and a process-led approach, Emulsion aims to create inspiring, comfortable and innovative environments that reinforce the core values of clients and its own practice.

Opposite: Rock Vault, a jewellery exhibition for London Fashion Week at Somerset House, London. Display cabinets are housed in an installation of over-scaled crystalline elements.

Below: Bowden Street apartment, Kennington, south London. Stepped zinc-clad roof extension (bottom left). Living room with black steel and concrete fireplace (top). Galvanised steel and timber staircase to the roof terrace (bottom right).

Erect Architecture Led by Barbara Kaucky and Susanne Tutsch, Erect Architecture specialises in community architecture, play and public realm design, and user and stakeholder engagement with the aim of creating environments that people enjoy.

Narrative is central to Erect's projects, inspired by site, people and context. Projects include Timber Lodge and Tumbling Bay, a café and community centre within a playable landscape in the Queen Elizabeth Olympic Park. Kilburn Grange Park Adventure Playcentre, designed on the theme of playing in and around trees, won a RIBA Award 2011. Erect's Promenade of Curiosities won an international competition to develop a public realm framework for Vauxhall in 2014.

The practice collaborated on the update of Supplementary Planning Guidance *Shaping Neighbourhoods: Children and Young People's Play and Informal Recreation*. Erect is also exploring the potential role of design in improving public health through pilot projects such as Camden Active Spaces and Lambeth Early Action Partnership.

Opposite and below: Promenade of Curiosities, winner of the Vauxhall Missing Link competition to improve the public realm in Vauxhall, London. Public realm framework (right). Permanent and temporary installations along the promenade (left).

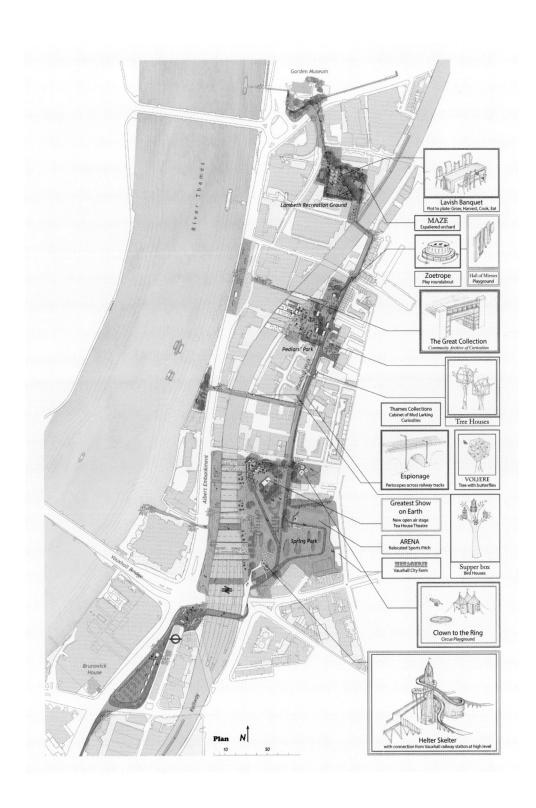

Kilburn Grange Adventure Play Centre and Playground. The play centre has an exposed timber-framed structure and biodiversity roof.

Queen Elizabeth Olympic Park North Tumbling
Bay Playground. Felled oaks support an undu-
lating net structure that gives way to treehouses,
tunnels and bridges intermingled with Scots Pine.

Feilden Fowles Fergus Feilden and Edmund Fowles completed their first building, the Ty Pren passive long house in the Brecon Beacons, while still studying for their diplomas. They went on to set up in practice in 2009, and have since worked across the arts, education, heritage and residential sectors.

Many projects deal with sensitive and complex settings. At Carlisle Cathedral, Feilden Fowles is re-instating The West Range of the 12th century priory as part of a new entrance and education space. It is also working on the Chatsworth Estate in Derbyshire and is designing a new gallery and visitor centre at the Yorkshire Sculpture Park near Wakefield.

Constructed in cross-laminated timber with sweet chestnut cladding, the Lee Building at the Ralph Allen School in Bath won a RIBA National Award in 2014. Another education project, The Fitzjames Teaching and Learning Centre at Hazlegrove School, won a RIBA South West Award in 2015.

Opposite and below: The Lee Building, Ralph Allen School, Bath. Constructed in cross-laminated timber, the building is clad in sweet chestnut.

South elevation (left). West elevation (right). Approach from the north (bottom)

Fitzjames Teaching and Learning Centre,
Hazlegrove School, Yeovil. South elevation
and courtyard (top). Interior sketch (bottom
left). Central resource space (bottom right).

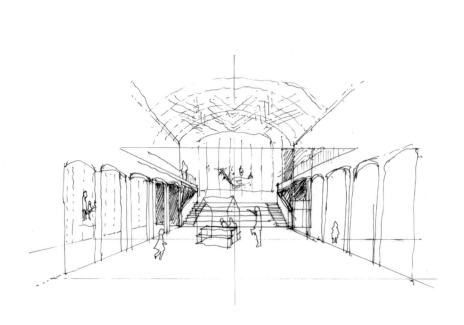

Yorkshire Sculpture Park visitors centre. The new low-rise building will be set into a hill-side at the southern entrance to the park.

Friend and Company

Set up in 2006, Friend and Company's work ranges from public realm to education buildings with a specialism in housing. Led by director Adrian Friend, the practice has a particular interest in how digital manufacturing can raise the quality of architecture and impact on design authorship. It is also researching affordable factory-made housing and new uses for high performance materials.

Housing projects include new builds and conversions. In Blackheath in south London, Friend's 21st Century Span House retrofit was based on a component concept of glass on the verticals and wood on the horizontals to achieve a stripped down modernism in tune with the Span original.

In De Beauvoir Town in north London, the Dray House project creates four new apartments clad in Portland Stone as a modest addition to the conservation area.

The practice has also completed several education buildings including a suspended 'treehouse' classroom at Chelsea Open Air Nursery.

Opposite: Dray House, north London. Four apartments clad in Portland stone make an unassuming contemporary addition to the conservation area.

Below: 21st Century Span House, south London. Concept model (top) for a systemised construction, prototypical glass and timber house. Replacement main staircase (bottom) with glass vertical and wood horizontal components.

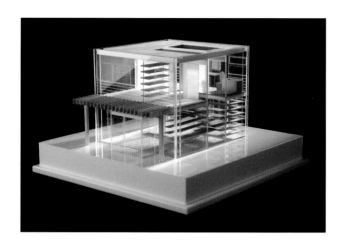

Gatti Routh Rhodes Architects

Based in East London, Gatti Routh Rhodes Architects was set up in 2013 by Richard Gatti, Stefanie Rhodes and Tom Routh.

Commissions include a new church and community centre for the Bethnal Green Mission Church. This proposes a double height church with basement and first floor community facilities plus key worker and private residential above. Completed work includes the conversion – with Matthew Lloyd Architects – of the Grade II listed St Mary of Eton church tower in Hackney Wick into a four floor apartment, and Out of the Ordinary, an exhibition of Korean architecture at The Cass gallery in Whitechapel.

Routh, who previously worked at Stanton Williams and Denton Corker Marshall, is a studio tutor at The Cass along with Rhodes, who is also a member of the RIBA Schools of Architecture Validation Panel. Gatti runs the Practice in the UK course for non-UK qualified architects, in conjunction with The Cass and the RIBA.

Opposite: St Mary of Eton, east London. Conversion of a Grade II listed Victorian Gothic church tower into a vertically-stacked residence.

Below: Bethnal Green Mission Church, east London. Accommodation is split between residential on the upper floors and church and community spaces on the lower floors. Exploded view (right). Facade study (left). Internal model view of the church (bottom).

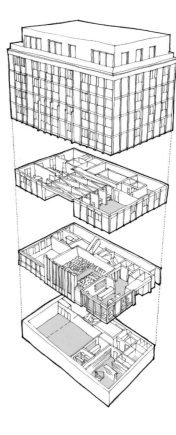

Gort Scott Jay Gort and Fiona Scott met while studying at Cambridge University and founded Gort Scott in 2007. The practice's diverse portfolio includes work across the leisure, retail, education, cultural, residential and urban masterplanning sectors.

A significant portion of its work has been for public sector clients. After carrying out research on the high street for the Greater London Authority in 2010, Gort Scott completed public realm renewal projects in Colliers Wood, Cricklewood and Bankside. The practice is part of the GLA's special advisors team and has completed further research for the authority on flexible workspaces and the regeneration of industrial areas.

Gort Scott is increasingly working for private sector clients, designing commercial offices for Jesus College in the centre of Cambridge, as well as Seafield House, built in local stone on the coast of the Isle of Man. Latterly the practice has worked internationally, designing The Rock, a large private house overlooking a lake in the Canadian mountain resort of Whistler.

Opposite and below: Offices for Jesus College,
51 Hills Road, Cambridge.

Front elevation (left). Side elevation from
Claremont, a collection of model houses (right).
Office interior (bottom).

The Rock private residence, Whistler,
Canada.

Model overview looking south (top) showing
the rocky outcrop site. Model view kitchen/
living spaces (bottom).

Wembley Public Toilets and Public Realm, north London.

The pavilion's generously day-lit interior is animated by dappled light from the filigree clerestory (top). The building glows when illuminated from within (bottom).

Graeme Massie Architects

Graeme Massie Architects Based in Edinburgh, Graeme Massie Architects works broadly from masterplanning and architecture to product design and public art, with projects in mainland Europe, China and the Middle East as well as in the UK.

The practice has had considerable success in open international competition. In Iceland, it won contests for both the masterplanning of the Old Harbour and the redevelopment of the former airport at Vatnsmyri in Reykjavik, as well as the competition to masterplan the town centre of Akureyri in the north of the country.

In Oxford, Graeme Massie Architects won the RIBA international competition to refurbish Bonn Square for formal and informal civic events. The design included bespoke bronze furniture and an articulated stone surface and was completed in 2008. The practice won the Centenary Square landscape competition in Birmingham in 2015.

Both founder Graeme Massie and director Stuart Dickson teach at the Mackintosh School of Architecture in Glasgow.

Opposite and below: Bonn Square, Oxford.
The square has been transformed into a venue
for informal and formal civic events (left).

Plan (right) showing the new articulated
stone surface, steps and lighting masts.
Paving textures (centre).

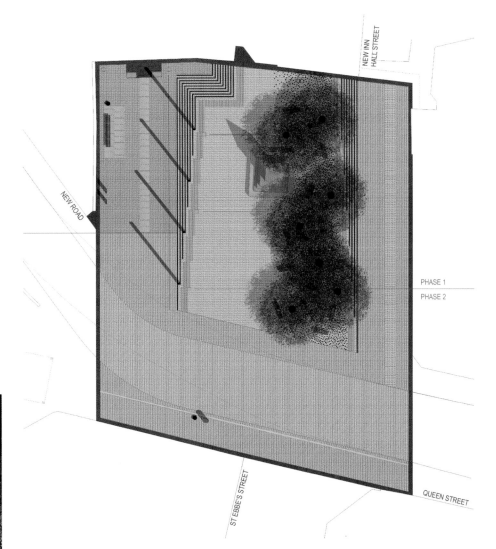

Centenary Square, Birmingham. Known as the
Hall of Columns, the design was the winning
entry in an international competition to redesign
the square.

Old Harbour, Reykjavik, Iceland. This competition-winning scheme proposes a new peninsula
(top) as part of plans to transform the waterfront
into a new public space alongside its active port.

Old Harbour urban plan (bottom).

Hall McKnight Based in Belfast and London, Hall McKnight was established in 2010 by Alastair Hall and Ian McKnight.

Much of its work involves public buildings and spaces with many commissions won through international design competition. In 2012, Hall McKnight won a RIBA contest for the Quadrangle Building at King's College's Strand campus in central London.

At Vartov Square in Copenhagen, the practice created new public space adjacent to the City Hall, a design that was shortlisted for The European Award for Architectural Heritage Intervention in 2015. Its Yellow Pavilion in Lewis Cubitt Square at King's Cross, was designed to promote Irish Design at the 2015 London Festival of Architecture.

Hall McKnight also designs individual houses and housing. Projects include a social housing block overlooking the River Foyle in Derry.

The practice was previously Hackett Hall McKnight, architect of Belfast's MAC Arts Centre which won the Architectural Association of Ireland's 2013 Downes Medal for architectural excellence.

Opposite and below: Social Housing, Derry, Northern Ireland. Site plan (right) showing location next to the river Foyle. Study model (bottom). Perspective image from Craigavon Bridge (left).

Overleaf: Large scale study models for Social Housing, Derry (right) and Kings College, London (left).

Proposed tower for Kings College, London on its
Strand Campus, viewed from Fountain Court.

Vartov Square, a sequence of new public spaces
adjacent to the City Hall in Copenhagen. Site plan
(top). Aerial photo (bottom).

Haptic Architects As suggested by its name, Haptic Architects is interested in the sense of touch, placing a particular emphasis on the quality of user experience in its buildings. The practice was established in 2009 and is based in London and Oslo.

Projects include airports, hotels, conferencing facilities, masterplans, mixed-use residential, exhibition spaces and private dwellings.

Designs are inspired by nature. In Norway, a project for a mountain lodge at Sognefjorden is designed to give optimum views of the fjord and mountains, grouping five pitched roof buildings around a central space. Each lodge is clad internally and externally in timber. In the Czech Republic, the Oaks housing project is oriented to optimise garden and interior sunlight as well as views of the countryside.

Infrastructure projects include Istanbul Grand Airport, where Haptic is working as part of the Grimshaw-led team. The practice is also masterplanning and designing key buildings at Straume town centre in Norway.

Opposite: Mountain lodge, Sognefjorden, Norway. Inspired by the traditional Norwegian farmstead, the hotel is formed by five buildings grouped around a central courtyard.

Below: Oaks Prague, Czech Republic. Model (top) showing houses clustered around a semi-private courtyard. Communal courtyard (bottom).

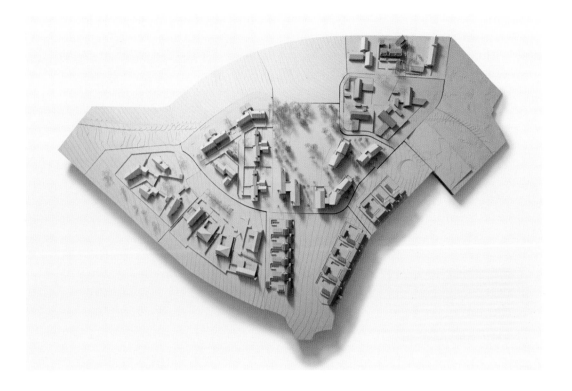

HAT Projects Founded by Hana Loftus and Tom Grieve in 2007, HAT Projects made its
name as designer of the RIBA Award-winning Jerwood Gallery in Hastings.

Based in the Essex town of Colchester, the practice has a focus on cultural, workspace
and civic projects and, increasingly, rural housing. Aside from the Jerwood Gallery, its most
significant completed project is High House Artists' Studios, a complex of new-build affordable rent studios in Purfleet. This won a RIBA Award in 2014 and led to HAT being named
RIBA East Emerging Architect of the Year.

Further clients include the Victoria and Albert Museum, the Gasworks gallery and studio
complex in south London, and the National Skills Academy for Creative and Cultural Skills.

HAT is active in its locality as a community enabler, design adviser and self-builder,
advising its local authority on cultural development and building an outdoor classroom for its
local school. It places particular importance on experimentation through hands-on making.

Opposite and below: Jerwood Gallery, Hastings. The gallery (left) is situated on the Stade between the medieval part of the town and the working fishing beach. Temporary exhibition space (right). Model (bottom).

High House Artists' Studios, Purfleet (left). Main staircase (right). The affordable rent complex won an RIBA Award in 2014 and led to HAT Projects being awarded RIBA East Emerging Architect of the Year.

Gasworks gallery and studio, south London.
New street facade (bottom) and interior (top).

Hayhurst and Co has built almost 40 projects since it was established in 2009.
  The practice has developed a particular specialism in school design, completing
a number of school expansions including Pegasus Academy in Croydon, which created
seven new classrooms through a series of interweaving interventions and extensions.
In the same borough, the practice's expansion of Hayes Primary School won New London
Architecture's best overall Building of the Year Award in 2013. Further projects include
Edith Neville Primary School, a new build school in central London.
  Housing and one-off houses are another focus. The practice won RIBA London Small
Project of the Year Award in 2012 for its slate-clad, green-roofed Hairy House extension.
Hayhurst and Co is increasingly working at a larger scale and is designing a number of indi-
vidual new build properties including a house and studio behind a Victorian terrace
in Hackney, London.

Opposite and below: Pegasus Academy, Croydon. The new extension (left) responds to the pitches and massing of the existing Victorian school buildings.

Site axonometric, with differently scaled roof pitches (bottom). Nursery teaching space with ply-lined ceilings (top).

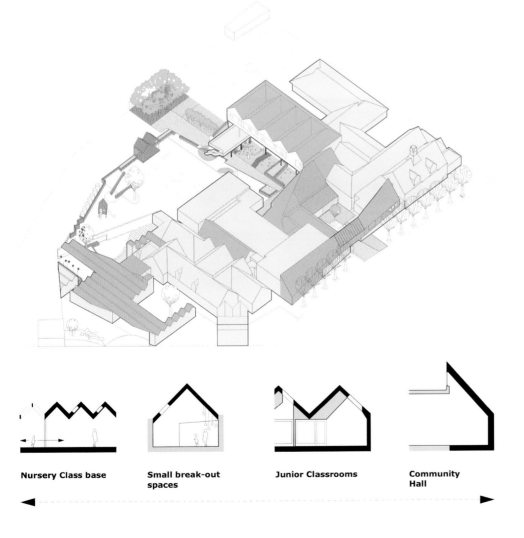

Nursery Class base

Small break-out spaces

Junior Classrooms

Community Hall

Hayes Primary School, Croydon. New main entrance, with mirror polished stainless steel screen (top).

Timber construction axonometric showing cross-laminated timber elements and timber shingle cladding (bottom).

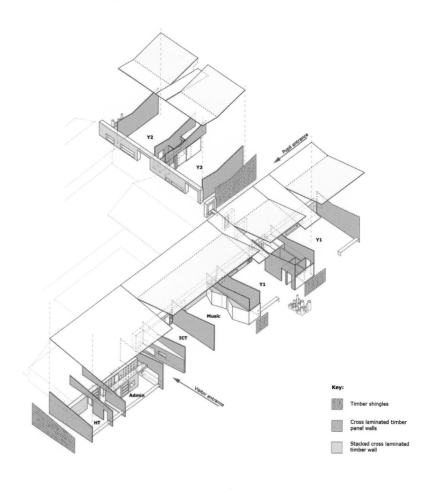

Key:

Timber shingles

Cross laminated timber panel walls

Stacked cross laminated timber wall

Hairy House, west London. Rear elevation of
a green-roofed extension to a Victorian House
in a conservation area in Hammersmith.

Hugh Strange Architects Established in 2011, Hugh Strange Architects won multiple awards for its first built project, a house and studio for practice founder Hugh Strange in Deptford. Made from pre-fabricated timber panels in a Swiss factory, the structure of the house was erected on site within a week.

Strange has a keen interest in innovative construction techniques, with a particular expertise in cross-laminated timber construction. Emphasis is given to practical solutions that are intended to be both cost effective and poetically conceived.

The practice works in sensitive rural contexts as well as inner-city urban sites. At Shatwell Farm in Somerset, commissions include an archive for architectural drawings, the conversion of two agricultural silos into a private library and model store, and a sculpted canopy designed in collaboration with renowned Portuguese architect Álvaro Siza. In the Avon Gorge near Bristol, it completed a timber cabin for staff and visitors, set within a new nature reserve.

Opposite and below: Architecture Archive, Somerset.

The new cross-laminated timber structure utilises an existing barn (right) and is used without internal lining (left and bottom middle). Site model (top).

Architecture Library, Somerset. Cutaway
model of new library housed within two
disused agricultural silos adjacent to
the Architecture Archive.

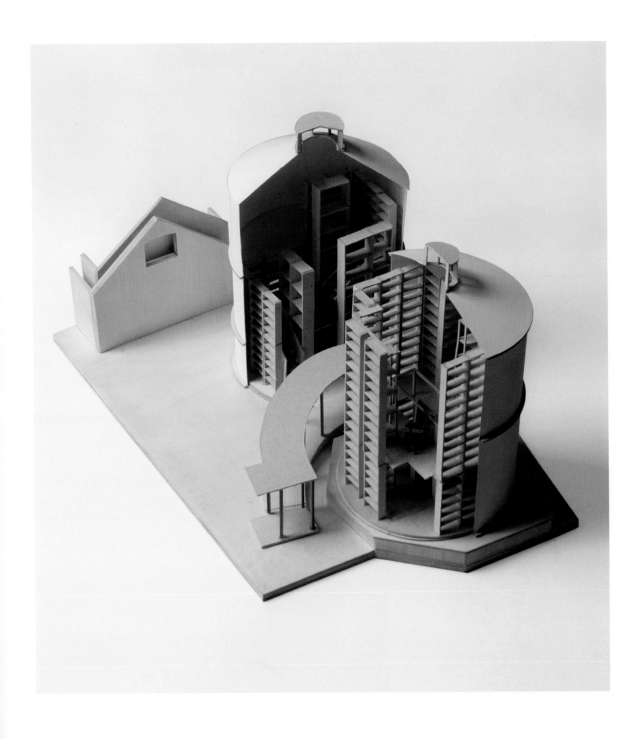

Clapton House, east London. This two storey terraced house was extensively remodeled. Living space (left). Rear facade (bottom).

Overleaf: Strange House & Studio, south east London. The house is sited in an old pub yard and is largely concealed from the street by an existing perimeter wall.

Hugo Hardy Architect runs his practice from Berkhamsted in Hertfordshire. He set up on his own in 2010 having worked for a number of London practices including Arup, Jonathan Tuckey Design and David Chipperfield. Previously, he studied in Canada and at The Berlage Institute in the Netherlands, and has also lectured at the Vancouver Film School.

Hardy has designed a number of domestic extensions, refurbishments and new builds as well as an artist's studio near the Grand Union canal in Berkhamsted. He describes his design approach as striving to 'uncover the essential character of a place and to express this in a considered manner for today'.

He has been shortlisted for several competitions including Europan 8 in Milton Keynes and The WC of the Future for Dyson. A competition entry design for a dual-purpose holiday let/cricket pavilion building at Coniston is conceived as a modern take on the Lake District vernacular.

Opposite: The Artist's Haven, Berkhamsted. Created in a derelict former coalman's barn, the existing brick shell is infilled with a braced timber frame to support a trussed timber first floor.

Below: Tithe Barn (Coniston Cricket Pavilion, Cumbria). The building is a dual purpose pavilion and holiday let. Axonometric (left). Model views (right).

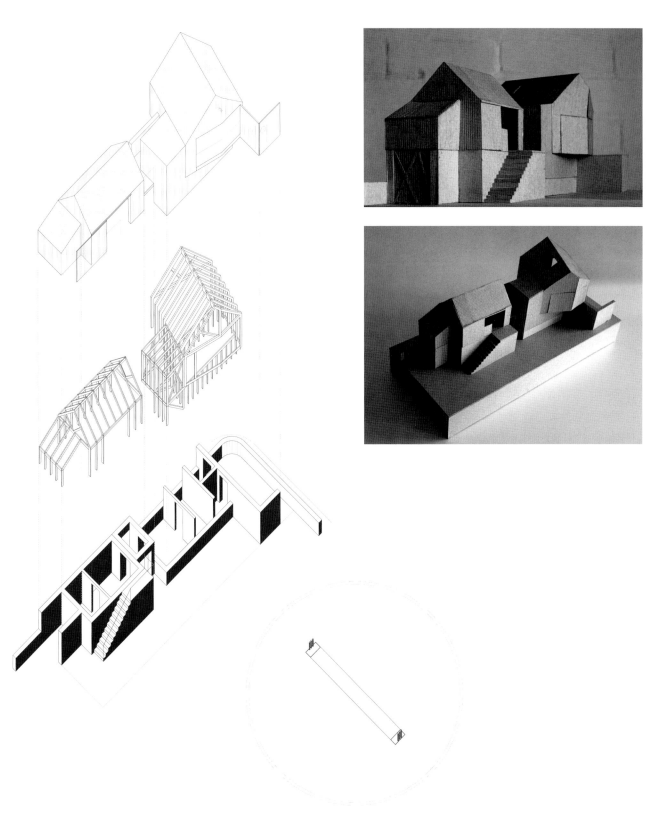

Invisible Studio Piers Taylor set up Invisible Studio in 2012 after six years with the
Mitchell Taylor Workshop. The practice regards itself as experimental, progressive, and
dedicated to collaborative ways of working and sustainable design. Its work ranges from
ecologically-sensitive self-builds through to schools, public buildings and large-scale
urban environments.

Taylor has a particular expertise in timber design, creating the large-span Big Shed
workshop at Hooke Park in Dorset with students from the Architectural Association.
His Moonshine self-build house was built using unseasoned timber in components that
had to be carried by hand to the site 500 metres along a woodland track.

The practice is based near Bath in Visible Studio, a woodland studio built by the
practice with unskilled neighbours and friends using untreated and unseasoned wood
grown on the site.

Taylor trained in Australia under Glenn Murcutt and has taught at the universities
of Cambridge and Bath and at the Architectural Association.

Opposite and below: Hooke Park Big Shed, Dorset.
Designed and constructed with Architectural
Association Design & Make masters students
(bottom). The larch roundwood primary structure
(right) is clad in western red cedar boarding (left).

Stillpoint, Bath. A new health clinic, martial arts dojo and housing designed to create a new urban space and re-link a number of former artisan courtyards (bottom). Dojo interior (top).

Visible Studio, Bath. The woodland studio was built for and by Invisible Studio using timber grown on site and other found and scavenged materials at a total cost of £15,000.

Jack Woolley worked as an industrial designer for many years before retraining as an architect and setting up in practice in 2009.

His work is particularly concerned with unlocking latent potential in existing buildings and sites. He won the Architect's Journal Small Projects Award in 2012 for his first completed project, the conversion of a derelict carpenter's workshop into a modern live/work space that doubled the habitable area by inserting an offset basement.

He has completed two separate new build houses on constrained sites on the former gardens of Victorian terraces. At Cardozo Road in north London, the partially subterranean house preserves long views across the site while drawing light into the lowest level. Spiral House in south London is a single-storey house conceived as one wall that forms the site boundary before spiraling round to create habitable spaces.

Several projects involve re-used materials including a shelter created from 600 used crisp packets.

Opposite: Crisp Packet Shelter, made using 600 used crisp packets washed and welded together.

Below: Spiral House, Balham, London. East elevation (top). Steps down to the house entrance (bottom right). Living area and kitchen (bottom left).

Jan Kattein Architects (JKA) specialises in housing, urban design, town centre regeneration and theatre design. Jan Kattein set up the practice in 2005 after working at Jestico + Whiles and Peter Barber Architects, where he was project architect for the Donnybrook housing project in Bow.

JKA has collaborated with shopkeepers on several high street regeneration projects including Leyton in east London and Croydon, Sutton and Nunhead in south London. In Stamford Hill, the practice is working on a regeneration strategy to help preserve the north London area's local identity at a time of significant population growth.

Housing is another key area. JKA was appointed to Peabody's small projects panel following its competition entry to design 20 new homes on Morpeth Road in Hackney. Its design proposed a terrace that generates a well-overlooked street while maintaining the privacy of courtyard gardens. Also for Peabody, JKA was commissioned to design infill development on Islington's Whitecross Estate.

Opposite: Caledonian Road, central London. A disused shop was converted into two flats and a commercial unit with a colourful blue and orange brick rear elevation.

Below: Morpeth Road, east London. Competition winning proposal to turn a row of derelict garages into a residential terrace (top). Doors, windows and courtyards open onto the pavement (bottom).

Jonathan Hendry set up his practice in Lincolnshire after working in London
for Jamie Fobert Architects, Allies and Morrison and the Architecture Research Unit.

The practice is interested in using simple, well-crafted forms to create a timeless
regional architecture that relates to landscape, geology, climate, site and use.

Clients range across the private, public and commercial sectors in the housing,
arts & heritage and community sectors.

The practice won an RIBA Award in 2012 for its Caistor Arts & Heritage Centre, a conversion of a former Methodist chapel. At Great Coates, it designed a Village Hall clad in black-
painted, vertical marine ply with a zinc standing seam roof that references the form of the
nearby church. A folly design for a site within the Lincolnshire Wolds Area of Outstanding
Natural Beauty draws on the Gothic character of a former nearby manor. Hendry is a former
studio master at Cambridge University, where he taught from 2011–14.

Opposite and below: Great Coates Community Hall, Lincolnshire. The hall stands on the edge of a paddock (centre top) and is clad in marine ply planks coated in black bitumen paint (centre bottom). Entrance hall (right). Main hall (left).

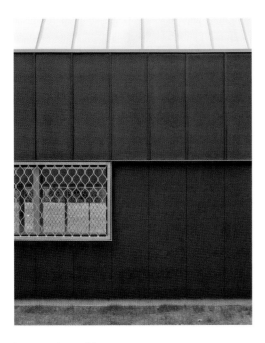

Caistor Arts & Heritage Centre, Lincolnshire.
The centre is housed in a sensitively restored
former Methodist chapel (left). Library (right)
lined with black paneling and shelves.

Moat Cottage Folly, Lincolnshire. Rendered
front elevation of the cottage (left), which replaces
a former gamekeeper's house. Plans (right).
Internal view (bottom).

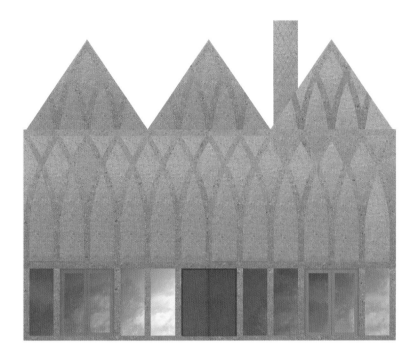

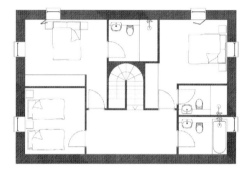

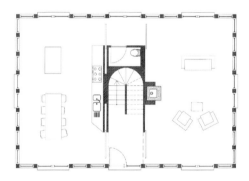

Laura Dewe Mathews has specialised in one-off residential projects since establishing her London-based practice in 2010.

Her first new build was Gingerbread House, a one-bed house on the site of a former box factory in Hackney, east London. Designed for herself, the 80sq m house has a cross-laminated timber structure and is covered with distinctive cedar shingles inspired by decorative Russian vernacular architecture. The house won several awards including the Architect's Journal Small Projects Award and the Grand Designs Small Project Award in 2013. Her portfolio has recently diversified to include a farmhouse and studio in Cambridgeshire, a new-build house with artists' studios and workshop for a young family in Provence, and a bothy in the West Country.

Dewe Mathews trained at the Bartlett School of Architecture and worked for Block Architecture and Waldo Works in London and Peter Stutchbury Architects in Sydney before setting up on her own.

Opposite and below: Gingerbread House, east London. Exterior, with the new cedar-clad form emerging from within the original workshop brick walls (top right).

Cladding detail (bottom left). Kitchen leading to private courtyard (far left). Open plan kitchen/dining/living space (bottom right).

Liddicoat & Goldhill

Liddicoat & Goldhill David Liddicoat and Sophie Goldhill met at the Royal College of Art and set up in practice in 2009 in east London. Initially, Liddicoat & Goldhill worked as its own client on low-cost, compact domestic architecture, completing the RIBA Award-winning Shadow House near King's Cross in Camden, London in 2011.

The practice has since worked on many private houses including the Ancient Party Barn, a conversion of a seventeenth century granary and threshing barn in Kent which won a RIBA award in 2015. In Essex, Thousand Trees House is designed to merge with the canopies of nearby trees.

Liddicoat & Goldhill has also diversified into public and commercial work, winning the Architecture Foundation's Barkingside streetfront competition and working with retailer TM Lewin on the RIBA Regent Street Windows installation. International projects include a new national cricket facility in Sierra Leone, micro-hotels in Mozambique and Kenya, and the Lux gallery/project space in Dublin.

Opposite: The Lux Gallery, Dublin, Ireland.
Liddicoat Goldhill is adapting and extending
a city centre warehouse as a new venue for
a private contemporary art gallery and café.

Below: The Thousand Trees House, Essex.
The form refers to the rolling topography
of the site and merges with the canopies of
nearby trees. (top). The roofs and floors will be
constructed using reciprocal frames (bottom).

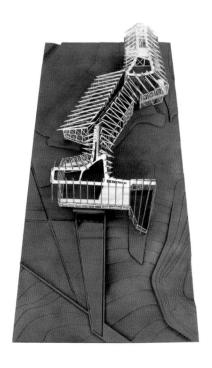

Lyndon Goode Architects

David Lyndon and Simon Goode established their London-based practice in 2012. Lyndon previously worked at Haworth Tompkins, where he completed the new campus in Battersea for the Royal College of Art (RCA), while Goode led the design team for the King's Cross station redevelopment while at John McAslan & Partners.

Lyndon Goode works mainly in the housing, cultural and community sectors. The practice is developing affordable housing for Peabody at Fish Island in Hackney Wick and compact dwellings for Pocket Living in the UK. It is also working on affordable housing for the United Nations and international diplomatic group The Office of the Quartet.

Community projects include the regeneration of 12 high street shopfronts in Archway for the London Borough of Islington. Cultural clients include the Royal Court Theatre and the RCA.

The practice aims to make its clients' assets more attractive and successful through architecture that is 'audacious, surprising and playful'.

Opposite: The Cedar House, Chelsea, central London. Roof terrace, with turrets salvaged from the Victorian studios that originally occupied the building.

Below: Fish Island, Hackney Wick, east London. Competition-winning housing proposal for Peabody designed to add to the vibrancy of the area (left) with generous connections to the public realm (bottom). Plaster cast fragment, (right) to test surface texture and pattern.

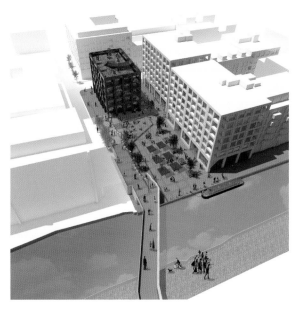

Matheson Whiteley

is a London-based practice led by Donald Matheson and Jason Whiteley, who established the studio in 2012 after meeting when working at Herzog & de Meuron.

The studio has a specific interest in the design of spaces for contemporary art and design. It was shortlisted for the 2015 RIBA London Awards for its creation of 610sqm of galleries, office and storage for the Stuart Shave/Modern Art gallery in Clerkenwell. In east London, its Mackintosh Studios project converted a disused commercial space into space for four artists.

Other projects include a new residence and studio for the designer Max Lamb, a canal-side atelier for the fashion label Peter Pilotto and a small painting studio on a loch-side site in Argyll, Scotland.

Among its larger-scale commissions are the residential redevelopment of a Hackney warehouse, and the design of a 20,000sqm workplace for media company Ogilvy Group within the Richard Seifert-designed Sea Containers House on London's South Bank.

Opposite: FischesNord public housing near Lake Lausanne, Switzerland. Prize-winning competition entry.

Below: Mackintosh Studios, east London. Three artist studios were created in the 1400sqm ground floor of an early 2000s mixed-use development.

Mikhail Riches
David Mikhail and Annalie Riches established Mikhail Riches in 2014. Both were previously directors of Riches Hawley Mikhail (RHM) and David Mikhail Architects.

Mikhail Riches is carrying on RHM's long expertise in housing. Its first project was the RIBA Award-winning Church Walk, where it acted as client, architect and developer for four houses and flats on a brownfield site in Hackney.

In Hackney Wick in east London, the practice is designing a £12million mixed-tenure building of approximately 50 homes, plus 1500m² of commercial space. It is also designing 105 Passivhaus homes (won as RHM) for Norwich City Council near the city centre and 50 homes on a prominent Tyneside site for Igloo Regeneration.

The practice is also expanding into other sectors through mixed-use projects such as a religious community in Streatham, south London, which incorporates a nursery and café. A proposal for a new quadrangle for New College Oxford includes new teaching and common rooms.

Opposite and below: Church Walk, Stoke
Newington, London. Mikhail Riches was client,
developer and architect for this scheme of two
houses, a flat and a triplex.

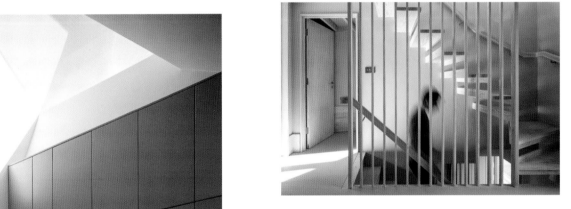

Brentford Lock West, London. Competition-winning scheme of houses and duplexes executed as Riches Hawley Mikhail. As many units as possible have their own front door.

St Margaret the Queen, Streatham Hill, London.

Models show proposals for the re-ordering of a Grade II listed church and grounds to include a new monastic house as well as new structures and spaces for community activities.

MW Architects specialises in residential design. Founded in 2009 by Matthew Wood, the practice designs both new builds and refurbishments.

Its best-known project is Essex Mews, a 2013 RIBA Award-winning development of three new houses in Crystal Palace, south London for developer Roger Zogolovitch of Solid Space. This design adapts the mews typology to modern lifestyles with an emphasis on space and connectivity. Communal spaces for eating, play and work are linked by half flights of stairs under double-height ceilings.

The practice describes its approach as back-to-basics with an emphasis on materiality, light and volume. Projects include a library pavilion on the South Downs and a copper-roofed gym in Hampstead. As well as its core residential portfolio, MW Architects has expanded into other sectors including commercial work. It recently completed Trio, a children's café, shop and workshop in Peckham, south London.

Opposite: Essex Mews, Crystal Palace, south London. Gable end elevation expressing internal split section of one of the three new build houses in the development.

Below: Cecilia Road Dalston, east London. Rear extension to lower ground floor maisonette. Side elevation (bottom). View through shower and study (left). Copper shower vent door detail (right).

Nex Set up in 2008 by Alan Dempsey, Nex Architecture derives its name from the word nexus, meaning both a connection and a focal point. Its aim is to work collaboratively to connect people to place through 'experience-focused' design.

Current projects include the creation of a photography centre for the University of Brighton within a 1960s office building, and a new cafe and square for the Cadogan Estate on the King's Road. Here, the café's wall will form a sheltered colonnade before spiraling up to create a rooftop space with seating. Nex is also designing a new entrance building, galleries, restaurant and learning centre at the RAF Museum in Hendon.

Completed work includes the Times Newspaper Eureka Pavilion, inspired by the cellular structure of plants and designed with landscape designer Marcus Barnett (2011/12), and a pavilion in Bedford Square to mark the 10th anniversary of the Design Research Laboratory at the Architectural Association (2009).

Opposite: Cadogan Café, Chelsea, London.
An existing listed wall is extended and wrapped
to form a new café with ground floor and roof
garden seating.

Below: Architectural Association DRL10 Pavilion,
Bedford Square, central London. The pavilion in
use (bottom). Interior (top), showing the concrete
and steel digitally-cut structure.

Nissen Richards Studio works across architecture, exhibition and theatre design.

Established in 2010, the practice designs extensively for major cultural institutions. For the Science Museum exhibition Collider: Step Inside the World's Greatest Experiment, Nissen Richards brought together a team from the theatre world to produce an immersive environment that evoked entering the CERN Large Hadron Collider. For the British Museum's exhibition Beyond El Dorado: Power and Gold in Ancient Columbia, the practice used scenic techniques to create a colourful and textured space to contextualise the 300-plus gold objects in the show.

Housing is another area of focus. Projects include a nine-unit apartment block for developer QNewHomes in West Norwood, the conversion of a former Victorian school in Stoke Newington, a medium sized mixed-use scheme in Sydenham, and Harrold House, a new build house for a private client in Bedfordshire shortlisted for the 2015 RIBA East Awards.

Opposite: Refurbishment of the Lydia and Manfred Gorvy Lecture Theatre, Victoria and Albert Museum, London. The design of the cupola ceiling inspired a new decorative pattern to the timber lining that surrounds the space.

Below: The Way to the Sea, Aldeburgh Festival 2010. Installations through the landscape at Thorpeness inspired by the local 'House in the Clouds' landmark.

OMMX directors Hikaru Nissanke and Jon Lopez studied at Cambridge University and the Architectural Association, and have been working together since graduating. They are now both Design Fellows at Cambridge, where they run and teach a design studio.

Their London-based practice designs buildings, rooms and objects. Projects range across social housing, private residences, offices, public spaces, festivals, exhibitions, shops, furniture and fittings. Completed work includes the restoration and conversion of a derelict farm in Pembrokeshire Coast National Park and exhibition design for the British Library. OMMX is masterplanning Clerkenwell Design Week 2016 and is working with English Heritage on images that show the reconstruction of the ruined Rievaulx Abbey in North Yorkshire.

OMMX was placed third out of 400 entries for the Detroit Riverfront competition, organised by the American Institute of Architects in 2012. It has been invited to produce a proposal to extend the historic Begijnhof in Bruges, for a special edition of Dutch architectural magazine Forum.

Opposite: Garden Room, Canonbury, north London. A terrazzo extrusion forms the garden landscape, water feature, planters and new garden room.

This page: Begijnhof restoration, Bruges. Invited proposal to extend the Unesco world heritage site. The concept includes a white 'veil' and timber structure that defines a cloister and provides access for remedial work (left). Plan (right).

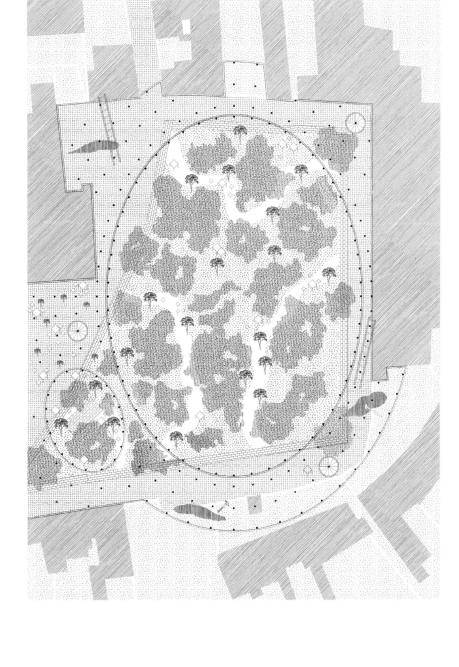

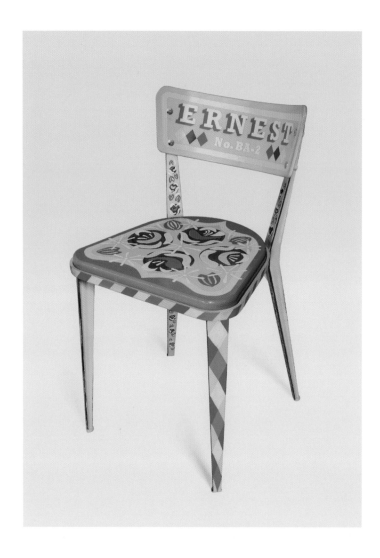

Ordinary Architecture was founded at the end of 2013 by former FAT director Charles Holland and Elly Ward, also previously of FAT.

The practice's name refers to its interest in popular culture, narrative and the creation of architecture that draws inspiration from the signs, symbols and spaces of everyday built culture.

While at FAT, Holland led the collaboration with Grayson Perry on the design of A House for Essex, the final stages of which Ordinary Architecture was novated to oversee. The practice has also completed two urban interventions in Los Angeles, both exploring its interest in supergraphics and pop iconography. Ordinary Architecture is developing designs for new rural housing in Wiltshire and a new build private house in north London. Ernest, a chair commissioned by Selfridges, is a decorative transformation of Ernest Race's classic BA-2 design of 1945.

Both Holland and Ward are involved in teaching, running studios at the Royal College of Art and University of Westminster respectively.

Opposite: Ernest, a re-working of Ernest Race's BA2 chair. Folk-art inspired hand painting creates a vibrant tension with the original's celebration of mass-production and industry.

Below: Private House, London. Perspective (bottom) and frontal axonometric (left) showing a white brick modernist building emerging from behind the facade of a London town house. Internal axonometrics (right).

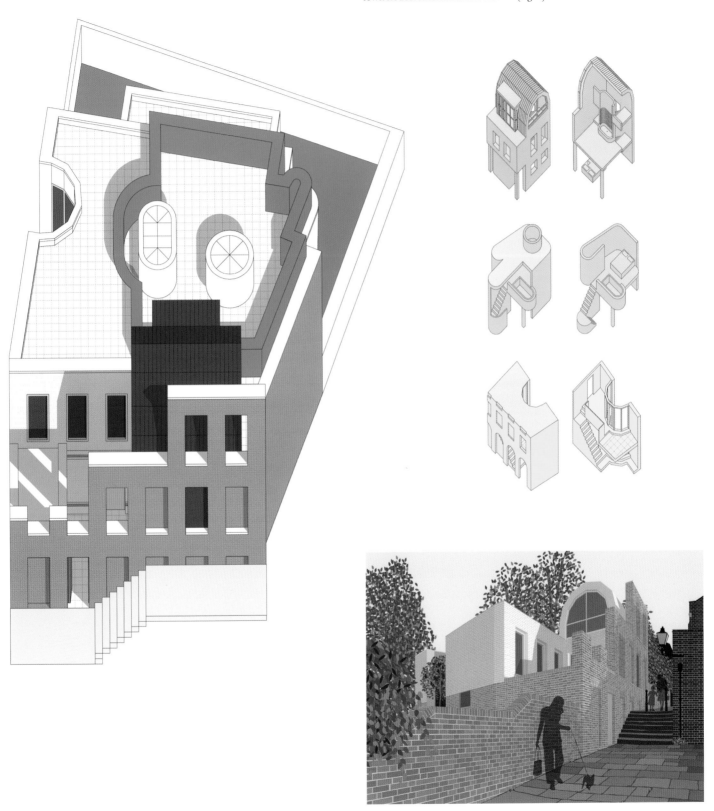

Orkidstudio is a humanitarian design organisation set up in 2008 by founding director James Mitchell, a lecturer in humanitarian architecture at the Mackintosh School of Architecture.

The organisation aims to use innovative architecture and construction to relieve poverty and promote sustainable social and economic development. Projects focus on both the process of design and construction and the final product as tools for empowerment and social change.

Orkidstudio has completed many projects in Africa including the £1k house, an affordable 60m² family home constructed from earthbags by a local workforce of unskilled women in Kenya and developed through a research programme at the Mackintosh. Earthbags were also used to build Nakuru, a 400m² children's home with bedrooms rather than dormitories, again built by locals in Kenya.

Schools include Swawou, a 1000m² girls' school in Sierra Leone, and Mutende II, a primary school in Zambia. Built in just seven weeks, this won the Royal Scottish Academy Medal for Architecture 2013.

Opposite: Mutende II, Zambia. Completed in seven weeks, the project delivered four large classrooms, an office and covered play space for a primary school.

Below: Swawow school for girls under construction in Kenema, eastern Sierra Leone (top). A local mason lays fired earth bricks (bottom).

Overleaf: Nakuru Orphanage, Kenya. Salvaged timber creates a tactile and protective facade that filters the light.

OS31 specialises in lightweight and adaptable architecture. Set up in 2014 by Tony Broomhead, Matt Pearson and Ross Jordan, the practice grew out of Broomhead's research into lightweight design at Sheffield School of Architecture, where he teaches.

OS31's first project, won in international competition, was a pop-up, fine-dining restaurant on ice made using scaffolding and tarpaulin. Located in Winnipeg, Manitoba in Canada, the temporary restaurant served 3000 covers in its 3-week existence in January 2015.

The practice also won a RIBA competition to design the Ask An Expert stand at Grand Designs Live in 2015, creating a wooden structure with cloisters around a central café. OS31 is moving towards being its own client, designer and contractor and is working on developing a pop-up restaurant in the UK.

Broomhead previously collaborated on public realm projects with Nicky Kirk as the practice Amenity Space, which also produced a radio show on the built environment.

Opposite: Winnipeg Restaurant, Manitoba, Canada. External render of RAW: almond, the first ever outdoor fine dining restaurant on ice, constructed using scaffolding and tarpaulin.

Below: Royal Academy of Arts, central London. Invited competition entry exploring movement and connection using an organic canopy that weaves through the building to link outside and inside spaces.

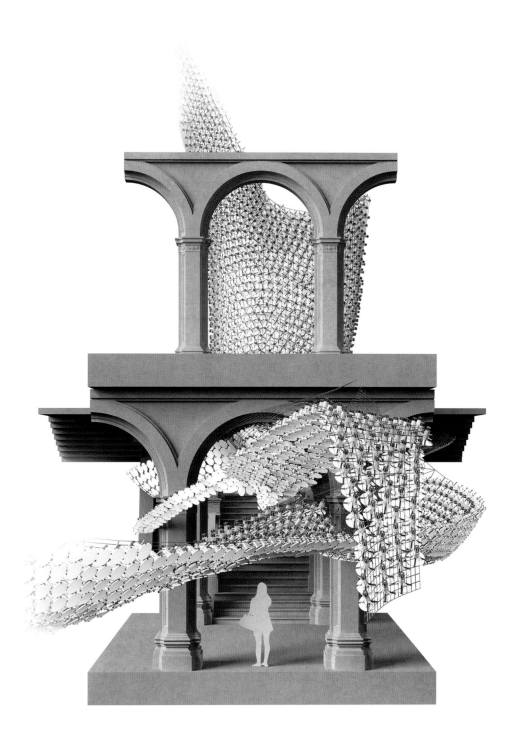

Platform 5 Architects' projects range in scale from a 'Shoffice' hybrid shed/office to the redevelopment of the LeSoCo further education college in Southwark.

Established in 2006 by Patrick Michell and Peter Allen, the practice works across the residential, commercial, education and cultural sectors. One-off houses such as the Backwater house on the Norfolk Broads are designed to relate to the local vernacular and landscape. Inspired by traditional Broads boatsheds, the house is raised above the waterline to allow floodwater to flow beneath a landscaped timber deck.

Recent larger schemes such as LeSoCo and the Ufford Street housing development in Southwark – which proposes 44 units in an apartment block and a mews – have enabled the practice to explore the design of streetscapes and public space.

Allen cites the practice's biggest challenge as 'striking the right balance between the needs of the practice as a business while still producing good architecture'.

Opposite: New open learning atrium at the Waterloo campus of Lewisham Southwark College (LeSoCo), London. The atrium has north facing rooflights and incorporates an overclad retained block.

Below: Ufford Street housing, central London. Early stage massing image (bottom) showing the potential for varied housing typologies. New pedestrian residential street (top) as part of the masterplan for the site.

Practice Architecture is a London-based design and build practice founded in 2009 by Lettice Drake, Paloma Gormley and Henry Stringer. The practice builds each project itself, often working with friends and volunteers and using low-tech materials and straightforward construction techniques. This approach, according to Practice Architecture, encourages a collective process of learning and exchange that shapes the design.

In Peckham in south London the practice created Frank's Café, a temporary summer venue on the roof of a disused multi-storey car park, using scaffolding boards, PVC and ratchet straps. The project was commissioned by not-for-profit arts organisation Bold Tendencies, along with an auditorium built out of barley straw. Further performance spaces include an amphitheatre for the New Art Centre in Wiltshire and the Yard Theatre in Hackney Wick.

Practice Architecture co-founded a community workspace in South Kilburn with the Architecture Foundation in 2011 and has also created a timber-framed self-build textile studio and home.

Opposite: Exterior view of Straw Auditorium, Peckham, south east London. Constructed from barley straw and OSB, the events space was built between the fifth and sixth floors of a multi-storey car park.

Below: Bench 1, New Arts Centre, Salisbury. Outdoor amphitheatre (top) built from scaffolding boards, steel and recycled plastic. Interior (bottom) used for workshops and education activities.

Below: Frank's Café, Peckham, south London.
Located on top of a disused car park, this restaurant and bar was built using scaffolding boards, tarpaulin and ratchet straps.

Prewett Bizley Graham Bizley and Robert Prewett founded Prewett Bizley Architects
in 2005. The practice has a particular commitment to reducing the impact of construction
on the environment, and strives to deliver low-energy buildings that are 'sensually engaging
and rooted in their particular context'.

The Dundon Passivhaus, Prewett Bizley's first new building certified to Passivhaus
standards, received an RIBA Award in 2015. Overlooking the Somerset levels, the house
has an envelope of green oak boards and uses a deeply overhanging roof to create sheltered
outdoor spaces.

Retrofits include the 80% House, a refurbishment of a Victorian terrace house in
a conservation area in Hackney that achieved an 80% reduction in CO_2 emissions in 2010.
In 2015, the practice completed the retrofit of a Grade II listed Georgian townhouse in
the Bloomsbury Conservation Area of London to EnerPHit principles.

Prewett Bizley are members of 15-40, an architecture collective that shares ideas,
knowledge and resources on retrofit and Passivhaus projects.

Opposite: Newington Green House, north London.
Ground floor living, kitchen & dining space
for new build house on a derelict site at the end
of a Victorian terrace.

Below: Dundon Passivhaus, Somerset. South-east
elevation from garden (bottom) and south (left).
Kitchen with snug and studio beyond (right).

Pricegore was established in 2013 by Dingle Price and Alexander Gore. The practice balances projects of modest size and budget with schemes at institution and city scale, such as the competition for the Helsinki Guggenheim. Both directors are involved in teaching.

Housing projects are a key strand of work. In House for a Painter, Pricegore erected a two storey residence within an artist's warehouse studio to create a live-work unit. In the Golden Hill housing project in Wiveliscombe, Somerset, an infrastructure of ground works, party walls, and principal facade enables householders to customise a range of standard types.

Another focus is projects for artists and creative organisations. At Studio House in Hackney, east London, Pricegore referenced the Smithsons' Hexenhaus project in pragmatic improvements including a new communal kitchen and courtyard. The practice is also working on the conversion of former school halls into exhibition and events spaces for Nottingham arts organisation Primary.

Opposite: House for a Painter, London. Conversion of a former industrial building into a house and studio for an artist and their family.

Below: Studio House, London. Improvements to two artists studios, including a new communal kitchen and courtyard garden.

PUP London practice PUP focuses on public/community architecture and creating small, 'magical' spaces such as temporary pavilions.

The practice was set up in 2014 by Theodore Molloy, Chloë Leen, Steve Wilkinson after the trio had collaborated informally on competitions. In 2012 PUP's Streetscape Carousel idea was a winning entry in the Greater London Authority's Dressing London competition for the London 2012 Olympic/ParaOlympic celebrations. This resulted in five temporary pavilions showing locally characteristic architecture in silhouette form.

For the Warming Huts competition in Winnipeg, PUP's Paxton Folly entry proposed shelters made of cast ice panels textured to create a crystalline interior.

The practice has been appointed to refurbish Surrey Docks City Farm in Rotherhithe. This work involves reinstating an arson-damaged tower, refurbishing the education/function room and re-landscaping between the farm and the Thames Path. Further projects include a new build house and a series of woodland timber cabins, both in Wiltshire.

Opposite: Paxton Folly, Winnipeg, Canada. Made from cast ice, the shelter was designed for a frozen river skating trail in collaboration with artist Bálint Bolygó.

Below: Surrey Docks Farm, Rotherhithe, London. External view of river room orangery extension (top). Ground plan (bottom) of proposed mini public plaza and spill out from the new river room.

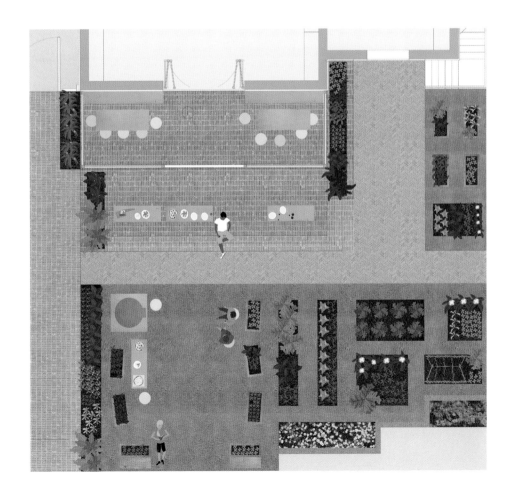

RA Projects Established in 2011 by Rashid Ali, RA Projects is a London-based architecture and design studio combining teaching, research and building. Ali studied at the University of Greenwich, the Bartlett (UCL) and the London School of Economics and teaches at University of East London. He is interested in pursuing ideas that respond to emerging spatial, social, and environmental patterns and conditions relevant to architecture and the city.

   RA Projects' portfolio is geographically-diverse, including UK residential projects, a boarding school in Somalia, planning and cultural strategies in African cities, and the design of the 1:54 Contemporary African Art Fair at Somerset House in London and in Brooklyn, New York. Work also varies widely in scope, ranging from a small-scale installation at the 2012 London Festival of Architecture to a strategic development plan for Maldives capital Male. Throughout, Ali aims to challenge the expected and familiar through creative use of design, material and technology.

Opposite: Fin House, central London. A sculptural blue steel staircase was introduced as part of a reconfiguration of this new three-storey house.

Below: Mogadishu – Lost Moderns, London Festival of Architecture, 2012. Exterior (top) and interior (bottom) of exhibition exploring Mogadishu through its architecture and urban environment.

RCKa aims to produce socially-responsive architecture that engages positively and meaningfully with those that use it.

The practice was formed in 2008 by directors Russell Curtis, Dieter Kleiner and Tim Riley after their win in the Europan 9 international housing design competition. Further community and residential sector work includes 40 starter homes in a refurbished Lewisham warehouse for developer Pocket Living, and four schemes for retirement developer PegasusLife.

The practice won a RIBA National Award and Civic Trust Award for the TNG Wells Park Youth Venue in Sydenham for Lewisham Council, for which the practice identified the site and helped secure community involvement and funding.

Other projects include the Open Eye photographic gallery on Liverpool's Mann Island and a Technology Centre for currency manufacturer De La Rue.

RCKa was a finalist of Young Architect of the Year in 2011 and 2013 and was named RIBA London's Emerging Practice of the Year in 2014.

Opposite: A Town in the Downs, south east
England. Masterplan proposal.

Below: Enfield Business Centre, north London.
The refurbishment included a new, flexible-use
entrance space (bottom). The new canopy
enhances the centre's presence on the street (top).

Previous spread: TNG Youth & Community Centre, Sydenham, south east London. Exterior view of west elevation from Wells Park (left).

Below: PegasusLife Harpenden, Hertfordshire. Detailed view of new retirement community for PegasusLife. The scheme comprises three buildings in a landscape setting.

Acoustitch, Waterloo Place, St James's, central London. Office reception installation created using foam wedges in a weave pattern (bottom). Development of the acoustic wedges (top).

Robin Lee Architecture   Robin Lee set up under his own name in 2011 after his former practice NORD split.

Based in London and Dublin, Robin Lee Architecture works diversely across public and private sectors with projects ranging from civic to utility buildings. Its aim is to create 'distinct spaces and places imbued with familiar qualities and atmospheres'.

The first project completed under his name was Wexford County Council Headquarters, awarded Best Public Building of 2012 by the Royal Institute of the Architects of Ireland. The building provides 11,500sqm of offices arranged as six blocks around a large, civic forum clad in Irish limestone.

Another major new build, The Confucius Institute, is due to complete in 2017 as a forum for Chinese-Western cultural exchange in Dublin.

In the UK, Robin Lee Architecture has designed a collection of utility buildings for the new North West Cambridge district, which is being developed by the University of Cambridge.

Opposite and below: Wexford County Council headquarters, Ireland. The exterior is wrapped in a double-skinned glass facade (top right).

Irish blue limestone clads the interior walls and floors (left). Central concourse (bottom), populated with large leather benches.

Queensway residence, west London. Conversion
of a former warehouse into a single dwelling
arranged across two floors. Upstairs (left). Stairs
detail (right).

Confucius Institute, Dublin. The building is conceived as a forum for the exchange of Chinese and Western culture. The ground floor is designed with strong connections to the landscape.

Roz Barr Architects is a London-based practice established in 2010 by Roz Barr, who was previously an associate director with Eric Parry Architects.

The practice works with a diverse group of private, commercial, retail and cultural sector clients. Projects range from a 500 ha landscape project in Granada through to a historic monument site in Loch Craignish Scotland, housing in London and a new showroom for Victoria Beckham in New York.

In 2012, Roz Barr Architects came second out of 750 entries in the Valer church competition in Norway. In west London, the practice is working on a landmark building for the Augustinian Order combining priory, church and art forum.

Throughout all, the practice aims to make interesting, innovative projects that respond to both client requirements and the cultural and historical context. Models and other three dimensional material form a key part of the early design process, with these often abstracted forms frequently becoming the foundation of the project.

Opposite: New Valer Church Competition (2nd Prize), Norway. Section model showing the domed main church space, formed with stacked blocks of larch.

Below: Pool House, Granada, Spain. The new building (top) is embedded in the arid landscape and becomes a route from the main house to a new terrace. Model (bottom).

Oculus, Store Street, central London. Aerial view of installation for the London Festival of Architecture 2012.

St Augustine's Church, west London. Proposed
new Augustinian centre and priory (top). 1:10
detail model for new priory (bottom).

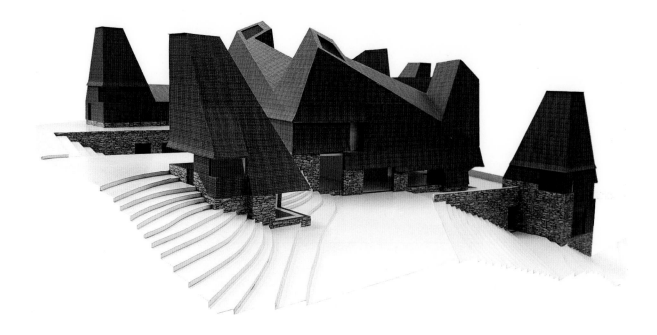

Rural Office for Architecture was established in 2008 by Niall Maxwell, who
runs the practice from a converted milking parlour on his farm in rural West Wales.

Classifying itself as regionalist, the practice focuses on developing contemporary
design responses to rural vernacular contexts. It works on residential and cultural projects
across the UK, and recently opened a London office to manage projects in the South East
of England. These include an extensive new house near Maidstone in Kent for the clients
to live with their three daughters and their families.

Rural Office for Architecture has won several RIBA Small Project of the Year Awards,
most recently in 2015 for the residential conversion of a Grade II listed tythe barn in Norfolk.
It also won a competition for a writer's shed at the National Writer's Centre in North Wales.

Maxwell is a tutor at the Welsh School of Architecture in Cardiff, and an Arts Council
Wales External Assessor.

Opposite: Private residence near Maidstone, Kent. Country home designed with James Wright for a client, their three daughters and their families.

Below: New Barn, Wales. Replacement barn (top) on the architect's farmstead. It is currently a temporary home while the rest of the farm is being redeveloped. Living space, heated by one of two Dutch tile stoves (bottom).

Russian for Fish Founded in 2006 by Pereen d'Avoine, Russian for Fish is a London-based practice specialising in residential architecture.

Completed projects include the Tapestry Court Penthouse overlooking the Thames in Mortlake. Here, the practice converted the second floor offices of a former public house into an open plan apartment and added a new rooftop extension.

For City View House in Tower Hamlets, Russian for Fish converted a studio flat into a one-bedroom apartment. Works included relocating the kitchen to beneath a new window to allow the creation of a new dual aspect living space. The mezzanine was extended with a new staircase replacing the existing access ladder.

In Brockley, south east London, the practice is planning to re-work a former light industrial site for a new use as live/work, combining new timber structures with retained brick facades.

The practice set up Russian For Fish Ironmongery in 2013 with the aim of producing affordable yet beautifully crafted ironmongery.

Opposite: Tapestry Court Penthouse and Pavilion, west London. One of two rooftop sunrooms created for new penthouse and first floor apartments.

Below: AM Live Work, Brockley, south east London. Proposed change of use from light industrial to live work, retaining existing brick facades (top) and introducing a new timber structure (bottom).

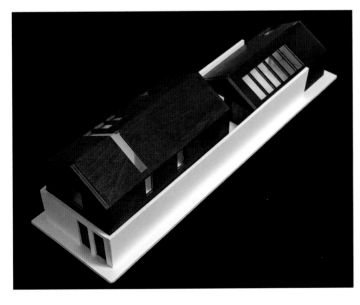

Sam Jacob set up his own practice in 2014 after 23 years as a founding director of FAT Architecture.

Sam Jacob Studio works across architecture, design and urbanism. The practice is focused on architecture's social and cultural significance and its relevance as a contemporary form of expression. Believing that architecture itself should be broad, the studio extends beyond the traditional role of architect to encompass research, strategy, criticism, curation, exhibition design, public art, and development.

Projects include a masterplan for 250 new homes in the South East of England that references strip farming field patterns to generate a new hybrid of urban and rural development. A public art project proposes siting a replica of an Avebury standing stone at the summit of Milton Keynes's Midsummer Boulevard. The studio has also designed a social hub for businesses and the wider community as part of a rethink of the traditional business park.

Opposite: Mixed use development in Shoreditch, east London. Self-initiated development combining a facility for a local community charity with a residential unit above.

Below: Cambourne masterplan, Cambridgeshire. Hybrid urban and rural development for 250 new homes. Massing and character study (top). Planometric study of housing/live-work/work units (bottom).

Sandy Rendel established his practice in 2010 after working as an associate at Tony Fretton Architects and James Gorst Architects.

Based in London, the practice has experience of both tight city sites and sensitive rural locations. Urban work includes the Old Cycle Club, a house and office created in a former church hall turned cycle clubhouse, and Thin House, a one bed house squeezed into a narrow terrace infill plot, both in Peckham.

Sandy Rendel's countryside projects include a new house on the banks of the river Ouse in the South Downs National Park and another on the edge of the New Forest National Park in Lymington, Hampshire.

Work is informed by an enjoyment of both traditional craftsmanship and modern technologies and materials. Rendel has lectured on construction at the University of Cambridge and the practice has undertaken a series of self-build projects that provide hands-on experience and a field for experimentation and research.

Opposite: Woodcock Lane, Lymington, Hampshire. View of a replacement dwelling on the edge of the New Forest National Park.

This page: South Street, Lewes, East Sussex. The new house is positioned on the banks the River Ouse (right) in the South Downs National Park. View from the approach to the street facade (top left). Construction photo of Corten expanded mesh cladding to roof and walls (bottom left).

Serie Architects is an international practice encompassing architecture, urban design and research on the city. Design is led from London by Christopher Lee, who founded the practice in 2006 in collaboration with Kapil Gupta, who is based in Mumbai, India. Serie has further offices in Singapore and Beijing.

The practice derives new architectural solutions from its study of historical building precedents. Competition wins have led to several of Serie's highest profile projects. In 2011 the practice won an international contest for the BMW London Olympic Pavilion with a scheme that used cascading water for evaporative cooling. Serie's winning entry for the Singapore State Courts Complex in 2012 splits administration and courtrooms into 150 metre-high linked towers. Also in Singapore, the practice won an open competition to extend the NUS School of Design & Environment, which will be one of the first zero energy buildings in the tropics.

Serie Architects won the Young Architect of the Year Award in 2010.

Aarvli Eco Resort, Goa, India. Construction photograph. The wavelike plan allows a sequence of punctuated circular openings that bring light into the building and allow the use of greenery and pools of water.

The Tote Restaurant, Mumbai, India. Conversion of disused buildings at the Mumbai Racecourse using a new structural system based on tree branches.

Singapore State Courts, Singapore. Physical model (bottom) of Serie's competition winning scheme, which splits administrative functions and courtrooms into two 150m towers linked by footbridges. Visualisation (top).

Something & Son is a London-based collective that works collaboratively across art, design and architecture on socially-driven and environmental projects.

Its FARM:shop installation turned a three storey Victorian terraced shop in Dalston, London, into a farm to discover how much food could be grown in an average inner London shop. This temporary arts project has evolved into a self-sustaining food community hub. Similarly Barking Bathhouse, an experimental, affordable spa in east London built for the Create festival in 2012, is still operational. They co-founded Makerversity, a maker community and learning space in Somerset House, which brings together start-ups with young Londoners.

The collective's diverse portfolio also includes Ek Biç Ye İç, a permanent indoor-out-door, public space and restaurant next to Taksim Square in Istanbul, a peat-heated Sweat Oratory for the Kinsale Art Festival in Ireland, and nests for migrating swifts in Cambridge in the form of an African setting sun.

Opposite: Sweat Oratory, Kinsale, Ireland. Sauna designed for the Kinsale Art Festival at the side of the bay.

Below: Barking Bathhouse, east London. Drawing (left) and exterior (right). The relaxation room (bottom) combines the communal nature of the bathhouse with a back-to-basics eco-industrial aesthetic.

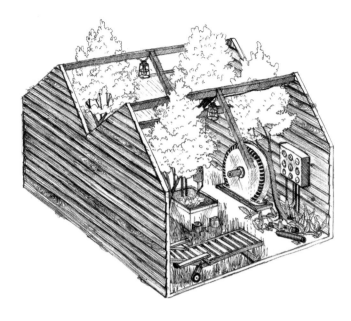

Stitch Founded by Sally Lewis in 2012, Stitch is a London-based practice specialising in housing and regeneration.

Stitch's vision is to create a new generation of great streets for the capital. The practice has advised on the design delivery of the 2350-home South Acton Estate masterplan in Ealing, west London and is designing two of the detailed phases of development of this previously failing estate.

In Walthamstow in east London, Stitch is working on the redevelopment of the Marlowe Road Estate, which will create 436 new homes, a playground, commercial space, and a public plaza for the wider community. In Dagenham, Stitch's regeneration of the Goresbrook Village Estate replaced three council tower blocks with more traditional streets of mixed tenure housing that integrate better with the surrounding area.

Before setting up Stitch, Lewis was head of urban design and masterplanning at HTA. She was shortlisted for the Architects' Journal Emerging Architect of the Year Award in 2015.

Opposite and below: Marlowe Road Regeneration, Walthamstow, east London. Bird's eye view (top right) of the proposals for an integrated new neighbourhood with a mixed use community plaza.

Physical model (bottom right). Visualisation showing reinterpretation of traditional terraced housing (right).

Studio Egret West Christophe Egret and David West set up their practice in 2005 with the aim of pursuing an integrated approach to architecture and urban design that brings 'surprise and delight' to place making.

Studio Egret West has since worked widely across the housing, education, culture, health, public realm and mixed-use sectors. Its masterplan and design (in collaboration with Hawkins Brown) for the rehabilitation of Sheffield's famous Park Hill estate was short-listed for the Stirling Prize in 2013.

The practice has completed a number of major mixed-use projects, among them Clapham Library in south London, which combines 136 apartments with a library and health centre. At the Erith Quarry development in Bexley, it proposes a combination of primary school, 600 dwellings and community facilities within a stimulating ecological setting.

Public realm work includes the Stratford Shoal, a kinetic sculpture of titanium and steel 'trees' that celebrate the entrance to Stratford Centre in east London.

Opposite and below: Park Hill, Sheffield. Masterplan for the refurbishment of the 1961 estate and the re-design of 300 of its duplex homes and commercial units.

Overleaf: The Fold, Sidcup. A curving, folded facade was used to break up the massing of the new housing and respond to the surrounding buildings.

Clapham One, south London. The mixed-use scheme provides a public library, leisure centre, a new gp surgery and residential accommodation.

Bath Western Riverside, Bath. Two residential pavilions on the edge of the River Avon sit either end of a new waterside park.

Studio Gil was established in London by Pedro Gil in 2008 and has since completed built and theoretical work in both the UK and Latin America.

Projects include installations, residential remodelling, commercial fit-outs, public realm and new education buildings and houses. Two that embody Studio Gil's international approach are Flex house, which was designed, drawn and modeled in London and built in Colombia, and the design of Plaza Latina, a Latin American festival in London for the Carnaval del Pueblo Association.

The practice's work is founded on the idea that good architecture is born out of methodology and process, and that its design can be intuitive and playful. Great importance is placed on craftsmanship, with extensive use of prototyping. Interaction between teaching and practice is also a priority.

Studio Gil's Concrete House, an extension of a Victorian terrace house in East London, was shortlisted for the RIBA London Awards 2015.

Opposite: Flex, Palmira, Colombia, 2009. External view of house from street.

Below: Toybox, London, 2012. View (top) and detail (bottom) of mobile installation. conceived as a giant toy box for children.

Studio Sam Causer describes its work as 'pre-occupied with the everyday and the intimate'.

Based in the Kent coastal town of Margate, the practice works across the areas of public space, private domestic, heritage, building conservation, cultural research and architectural activism.

Margate projects include the redevelopment of town centre buildings and spaces for art organisations Crate Space and Limbo Arts, and interventions into the RISK exhibition for Turner Contemporary. The 2015 installation Blushing Pavilion explored the potential transformation of abandoned seaside shelters in collaboration with Colombian artists Vividero Colectivo. The studio is also a founding member of the Margate Design Collective, a not-for-profit group of architects and urbanists focusing on sustainable culture, heritage and society-led development.

Elsewhere, completed work includes a Worlds End shop in Berlin for Vivienne Westwood and a design headquarters in London for fashion designers Self-Portrait.

Opposite: Blushing Pavilion, Margate, 2015. Temporary exhibition at an abandoned Edwardian shelter exploring the evolving role of seaside landscape and architecture. Created with Vividero Colectivo.

Below: Autograph House, north west London 2013. Extension and remodeling of a ground floor apartment. A new garden studio (top) is screened by silver birch trunks. Birch ply interior (bottom).

Studio Weave was founded in 2006 by Je Ahn and Maria Smith, who left in 2015. The London-based practice works mainly in the housing, education, arts and public realm sectors and is known for its narrative, idiosyncratic and often playful approach to design.

In 2014, the practice was a finalist in the Hans Christian Andersen House of Fairytales international competition, proposing a series of buildings planted in a subterranean garden. Its entry for the Tribeca Infobox competition in Liverpool in 2008 conceived an Inside Outside House with inner brick walls and exterior wallpaper.

Midden Studio, an artist's studio cantilevering over a stream in Kintyre in west Scotland, completed in 2015. Clad in patterned zinc, it references nearby vernacular buildings and the granite landscape.

Studio Weave is designing a centre for adults with learning difficulties in Kent as well as woodlands classrooms for a London secondary school for pupils with learning difficulties. The practice is also carrying out RIBA-funded research into co-habitation and shared living.

Opposite and below: Midden Studio, Kintyre. Artist's studio on the west coast of Scotland (left). The studio is cantilevered over a burn (right) and is covered in diamond patterned zinc cladding (bottom right). Plywood interior (bottom left).

Overleaf: InsideOutHouse – Design entry for the Tribeca Infobox, a house turned inside-out. The brick walls are on the inside while the wallpaper is on the outside.

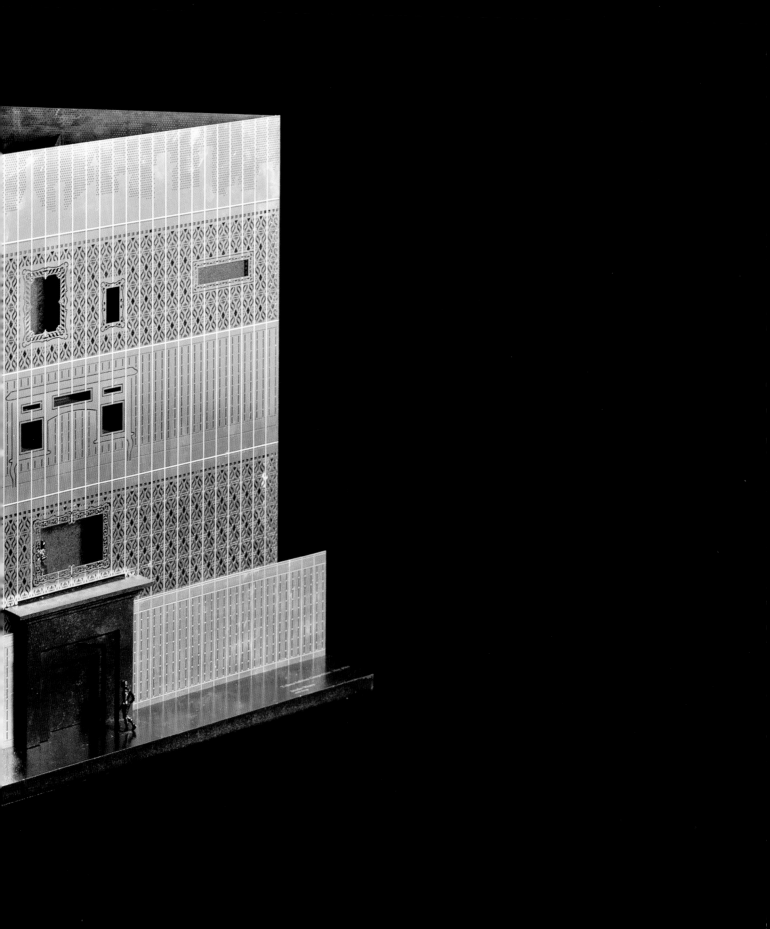

The Lullaby Factory, Great Ormond Street
Hospital. Central London. Installation (top)
for an awkward interstitial space.

Listening to Lullabies concept sketch (below).

House of Fairytales, Hans Christian Andersen
museum, Odense. Shortlisted competition entry.
Buildings (bottom) create ruptures in the earth
through which visitors can descend into an under-
world of magic and stories (top).

Surman Weston
Tom Surman and Percy Weston studied together at the Royal College of Art and set up in practice in 2014 after previously working as Weston Surman & Deane Architecture with Joseph Deane.

Weston Surman & Deane Architecture made an impact with its first two projects, a café utilising reclaimed materials for the RCA's Battersea Campus, and Writer's Shed, a garden studio for a writer and illustrator based in east London. Conceived as a fairytale hut at the bottom of the garden, this features cedar shingle cladding and was shortlisted for the AJ Small Projects Award.

Surman Weston currently works mainly for private residential clients but aims to branch out into the public realm and commercial sectors. Projects include an Islington garden studio clad in cork, which acts as both rugged rainscreen and insulation. Both principals teach as guest tutors/critics at various universities.

Opposite and below: Writer's Shed, east London. Night view of cedar shingle-clad shed (left), conceived as a fairy-tale hut at the bottom of the garden.

Interior book shelves, sink and stove (right). Illustration desk under north facing roof-light (bottom).

Self-Build on a Shoestring Competition.
Shortlisted proposal inspired by both the simple
construction techniques of Walter Segal and
pioneering digital fabrication technologies.

Configuration Diagrams

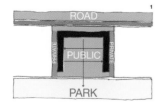 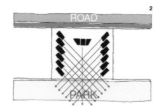 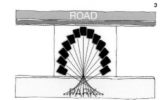 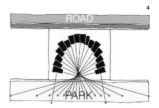

Construction process

Sectional Perspective

Royal College of Art Café, Battersea, south London. Located in the sculpture gallery, the café is conceived as a warm timber box within a stark concrete and steel shell.

Takero Shimazaki Architects (t-sa) aims to create 'timeless architecture with clarity and sensitive subtleties'.

Led by Takero Shimazaki, the London-based practice works primarily in the residential, cultural and workplace sectors. In Bloomsbury, central London, its design of a new six-screen art house cinema at the Brunswick Centre was inspired by the texture-rich films of Andrei Tarkovsky.

In south London, t-sa's conversion of a derelict office block creates 80 micro apartments aimed at key workers. In Leicester, it is turning a warehouse into studio/gallery spaces for Leicester Print Workshop.

The Centre for Sight, an eye hospital conceived as a series of barn-like forms, was completed in 2009 on the outskirts of East Grinstead. In 2014, the practice converted a Georgian townhouse in London's Soho from office to retail and residential use.

t-sa describes its core approach as working economically with what already exists by engaging deeply with the site context and the narratives of clients and users.

Opposite: Staircase at Curzon Bloomsbury, central London. Original columns and slabs were exposed to work with new materials such as bronze balustrades and Italian plaster in a conversion of the former Renoir into a six-screen art house cinema.

Below: New House, Chester Road, Manchester. Elevation (top). Pigmented plaster model (bottom).

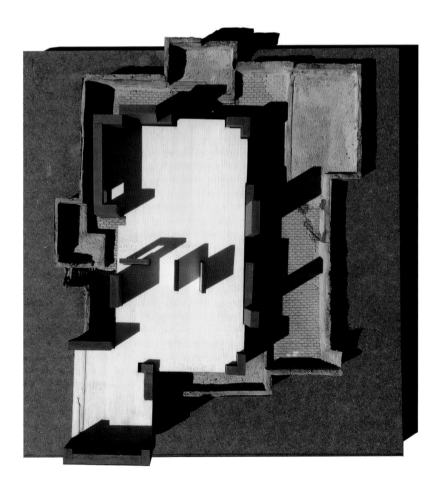

TDO architecture + design studio was founded by Tom Lewith, Doug Hodgson and Owen Jones in 2010 following a one-off commission from Wallpaper* magazine. The studio has since tripled in size, with projects in the residential, commercial, public and arts sectors ranging from £15,000 to £10million.

The three partners met and trained together at The Bartlett and work collaboratively on all projects. They work from a formerly disused railway arch in Southwark, London, which the practice renovated by inserting a suspended plywood workspace into an exposed steel lattice support.

TDO's Forest Pond House is a timber-framed meditation space/children's den that cantilevers over a garden pond. An integral bench looking over the water encourages reflection while the dark elevations serve as blackboards for drawings.

At Old Church Street in West London, TDO designed a contemporary infill house creating a brick elevation with hinged bronze ventilation panels and detailing in reference to the historic context of the terrace.

Opposite: Right To Flight, Peckham, south east London. One of three demountable pavilions designed for artist James Bridle's Right to Flight residency. Commissioned by non-profit arts organisation Bold Tendencies.

Below: Old Church Street House, west London. The street elevation (left) is a contemporary re-interpretation of the street's fenestration rhythm (bottom right). Patinated steel and smoked oak staircase (top right).

The Klassnik Corporation

The Klassnik Corporation's deliberately ambiguous name reflects the wish of architect and founder Tomas Klassnik to work beyond customary architectural remits.

As well as more traditional architectural commissions such as the renovation of modernist architect Peter Moro's former house in Blackheath, the practice works broadly across art, objects, installations and events. Projects include a temporary ping pong parlour in London's Soho, a scout hut frontage in Walthamstow, a touring shop for Puma inside a Luton van, landscape interventions for the London 2012 Olympic park, and most bizarrely, a séance to contact the spirit of Le Corbusier.

The Klassnik Corporation has been appointed to the Greater London Authority/Transport for London framework for public arts strategy and has worked on various public realm projects including new cycling infrastructure in Islington, public art in Barking and the transformation of the supporters club building for Cambridge United FC into a more diverse community space.

Opposite: Marsala Road, Lewisham, south east London. Terraced house renovation and extension. London stock brick provides continuity with the existing house, while zinc cladding encloses a new second floor loft and bathroom.

Below: 72 Rivington Street, Shoreditch, east London. New accommodation for creative agency YCN. A grey plywood ribbon forms desk surfaces at various levels and rises up to create storage space (top). Storage detail (below).

Timothy Smith & Jonathan Taylor aims to make creative modern buildings informed by the classical language of architecture.

The two founders, who have practiced together since 2009, teach a postgraduate design unit at Kingston School of Architecture, London, where Smith is also director of the BA Architecture course.

In addition to its core work of domestic extensions and remodelings, the practice has designed new builds and larger conversions in London and Yorkshire as well as art, cultural and housing projects.

Doug's Yard, a new house and barn conversion in Cambridgeshire, incorporates classical elements and draws inspiration from Sir Edwin Lutyens' late arts and crafts houses. Both Lutyens and Diocletian's Palace are referenced in another project at Lower Bryanston in Dorset, which includes a water tank grotto.

The practice is working on another barn conversion in the South Downs National Park. It aspires to create work that is both recognizable and unfamiliar using balance, proportion, character, intrigue and wit.

Opposite: Garden room and garden, Lower Bryanston, Dorset. Garden elevation, showing concrete framework infilled with textured brickwood.

Below: New house in Cambridgeshire. View from street (top) and garden elevation (bottom), with Cambridgeshire stock bricks, clay pantiles and stone dressings.

Urban Projects Bureau (UPB) works across architecture, urbanism, spatial strategy and design. The practice was set up in 2009 by Alex Warnock-Smith and Elena Pascolo, who are both course masters on the Architectural Association's Housing and Urbanism masters programme.

UPB has a particular interest in the way spaces are inhabited and a commitment to the public realm as a place of social exchange. Projects range in scale from events and exhibitions through to regional development strategies.

For Graveney School in south London, UPB created a 800sqm Sixth Form Study Block using Cross Laminated Timber and a polycarbonate facade.

Its Hard Working House project reworked and extended a run-down Georgian townhouse in London's Fitzrovia to provide a three storey family home with rooftop pavilion above ground floor commercial space.

UPB has participated in several major exhibitions including Venice Takeaways at the British Pavilion in the 13th Venice Architecture Biennale 2012.

Opposite: Graveney School Sixth Form Block, south west London. The 800sqm building is constructed from cross laminated timber with a polycarbonate front facade.

Below: A Hard Working House, Fitzrovia, central London. Lightweight rooftop pavilion created as part of a reworking and extension of a Georgian townhouse to provide a three storey family home above ground floor commercial space.

VPPR Architects describes itself as driven by the crossover of art and architecture. Based in East London, the practice was established in 2009 by Tatiana von Preussen, Catherine Pease and Jessica Reynolds and has worked on residential, public, commercial and urban projects in the UK, the USA and Russia.

The practice won RIBA London Awards for two new build residential projects with complex roof geometries – Vaulted House in 2015 and Ott's Yard in 2014. Vaulted House uses vaulted roof lights to admit light into the land-locked, former industrial site in south west London, while at Ott's Yard in north London, the triangular plans of the two houses are generated by the site geometry.

VPPR has designed various pavilions and installations including Foam Dome at 100% Design in 2014.

In 2015, it was named Emerging Architect and Emerging Woman Architect of the Year respectively by RIBA London and the Architects' Journal.

Opposite: Vaulted House, Hammersmith, west London. Vaulted roof lights bring natural light into this four bedroom family house, built in a former taxi depot.

Below: Ott's Yard, Camden, north London. Triangular skylights and planting (top) on the roofs of two new houses, created on a derelict infill site at the centre of a residential block. Dining area (bottom).

We Made That specialises in public projects. The practice was set up in east London in 2006 by founding partners Oliver Goodhall and Holly Lewis, who describe their work as demonstrating a 'dedicated civic ethos'.

The practice advocates the use of socially-engaged design processes to deliver relevant and accessible projects. In South Croydon, improvements to the public realm and building frontages included the temporary creation of the South End Ideas Shop. We Made That also produced the Croydon Meanwhile Use Toolkit, an online resource to encourage community groups to establish temporary uses independently of the local authority. Its five-week Open Office residency at the Architecture Foundation in 2013 explored various facets of neighbourhood planning in London.

As well as further high street improvement projects in Streatham and the Blackhorse Lane area of Waltham Forest, We Made That created the Wild Kingdom, a natural play space on Three Mills Green, Newham.

Opposite: Croydon South End, south London. Public realm and building frontage improvements in South Croydon's restaurant district.

Below: Wild Kingdom Playspace, Three Mills Green, Newham, east London. Illustrative overview (top). The playspace includes natural and reclaimed timbers, clearings, ridges and clamberable canopies (below).

West Architecture Graham West started out as a structural draughtsman at Ove Arup before training as an architect and setting up his practice in 2006.

West Architecture's first completed project, the Bavaria Road live/work studio refurbishment in Islington, involved the creation of a suspended timber mezzanine and won a 2006 Wood Award. In 2014 the practice completed Fitzrovia House, a reworking and extension of a bomb-damaged Georgian house in central London.

West Architecture works from a former Victorian workshop in Camden which it converted and now manages as a workplace for creative companies. The practice's workload is now 50% residential and 50% commercial. Since 2007, it has acted as executive architect on projects for Barworks. As well as pubs, these include the reworking of the ground floor of Keltan House, a 1960s office building in Hackney, to change it from cellular offices to restaurant/retail use.

West Architecture also created a temporary installation to mark Dover Street Market's 10th anniversary in 2014.

Opposite: Dover Street Market – The Next 10 Years, Mayfair, central London. Temporary installation to mark the store's 10th birthday. The structure visually screens the shop whilst encompassing the full width of the pavement.

Below: Fitzrovia House, central London. As part of a reconstruction of the house and workshop, a new link structure connects the workshop to the main house and completes the courtyard (top). Detail of courtyard glazing (bottom).

William Matthews set up his practice in 2013 after nearly 20 years at Renzo Piano Building Workshop, where he led the Shard design team.

Based in London, William Matthews Associates has worked over diverse scales ranging from a handcrafted kayak for Wallpaper* magazine to a feasibility study for a £600m office development in the City of London.

In 2014 the practice won its first international competition – the renovation of the Union of Bulgarian Artists' 1970s headquarters in central Sofia. Its design replaces the pre-cast concrete facade with glass largely covered in a white enamel screen print.

For Portland Street Hospital in London, William Matthews Associates proposed a suspended glazed walkway encased in a lattice exoskeleton to create an urban sculpture as well as a linking structure.

Further projects include a 240sqm cliff-top house near Dover, a two storey extension to London Bridge Hotel and a café pavilion in Canada Square for Canary Wharf.

Opposite: Canning Town Tower, east London. Visual for a competition for 250–300 residential units. The proposal puts all the units in a single 50 storey tower with six apartments per floor.

This page: Portland Hospital Footbridge, central London. As well as linking two hospital buildings, the proposed walkway is conceived as an urban sculpture which would delight passers-by (right). Model (left).

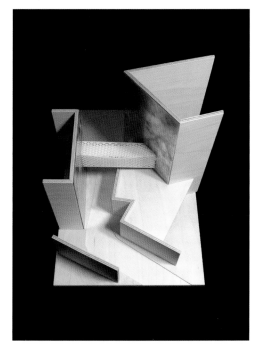

William Smalley established his office in London in 2010. The practice aims to provide 'memorable spaces of strong materiality'.

Private residential projects include the refurbishment of an apartment within an Alfred Waterhouse-designed listed building in central London, and the rehabilitation of an old stone farmstead in Oxfordshire in collaboration with Smalley's previous practice James Gorst Architects.

In the New Forest, the practice is designing a grass-roofed pool house within a Kim Wilkie-designed landscape. This proposes the use of black concrete to create the character of a natural rock pool beneath a great stone ledge.

In addition to residential projects, William Smalley has extended a south London nursery school and is converting a number of listed, former tannery buildings into offices and workshops in rural Wiltshire.

The practice's entry for the Guggenheim Helsinki competition proposed a cluster of zinc-clad galleries alongside a new public park with the aim of improving connections between the city and the sea.

Opposite: London apartment. Ploughshares from the client's country farm were accommodated in this refurbishment of an apartment within a listed Alfred Waterhouse building.

Below: Nursery school, south London. Zinc-clad rear extension with new outdoor reading and performing space (bottom). External staircase (top).

YOU&ME Set up in London and Athens by architects Alicja Borkowska and Iris Papadatou, YOU&ME explores how architecture, art and the public realm can be combined to create animated and loved public spaces.

This multi-disciplinary architecture practice is interested in heritage-led regeneration and how urban environments such as high streets can gain a local identity and new sense of place with the help of community participation. Projects include improvements to seven shops in Barking Town Centre as part of the Paint the Town regeneration programme. In Tottenham in north London, the practice is working on the refurbishment of more than 25 shopfronts along with associated public realm seating and artwork. It is also working on a heritage-inspired, public realm installation in Doha after winning the Old Doha Prize in collaboration with Qatari architects.

YOU&ME emphasises teamworking and collaboration with the aim of creating bespoke, adaptable and playful designs.

Opposite: Community workshop, West Green Road Haringey, north London. The workshop collaged a four-metre long map of West Green Road that informed artwork along the high street.

Below: Improvements to Tottenham High Street, north London. Artwork inspired from local stories of the Seven Sisters name (bottom right). Restored Victorian shopfront (top right). Bright new shopfront for a party shop (left).

Directory

31/44 Architects
Unit 101
3–15 Whitechapel Road
London E1 1DU
020 3735 7820
3144architects.com

A449 Ltd
23 Morton Street
Edinburgh EH15 2HN
0131 563 5152
a449.co.uk

ACME
76 Tabernacle Street
London EC2A 4EA
020 7251 5122
acme.ac

Adam Khan Architects
45 Vyner Street
London E2 9DQ
020 7403 9897
adamkhan.co.uk

Adam Nathaniel Furman
Unit 11
68 Broadwick Street
London W1F 9QZ
adamnathanielfurman.com

Amin Taha Architects
2/F, 12–13 Clerkenwell Green
London EC1R 0QJ
020 7253 9444
amintaha.co.uk

AOC Architecture Ltd
49 Columbia Road
London E2 7RG
020 7739 9950
theAOC.co.uk

Archipelago Architects
Unit 7
1 Old Nichol Street
London E2 7HR
020 7193 2714
archipelago-architects.co.uk

Architecture 00
109B Mare Street Studios
203–213 Mare Street
Hackney
London E8 3QE
020 7739 2230
architecture00.net

Article 25
One Canada Square
Canary Wharf
London E14 5AB
020 3197 9800
article-25.org

Asif Khan Ltd
1–5 Vyner Street
London E2 9DG
020 8980 3685
asif-khan.com

Assemble
Sugarhouse Studios
Unit A2
107 High Street
Stratford
London E15 2QQ
020 8221 2221
assemblestudio.co.uk

AY Architects
Studio 23
Bickerton House
25–27 Bickerton Road
London N19 5JT
020 7272 8899
ayarchitects.com

Baxendale Design Co. Ltd
De Anderen Studios
3 Osborne Street
Saltmarket
Glasgow G1 5QN
0141 552 1913
baxendale-dco.com

Bell Phillips Architects
First Floor
43 Tanner Street
London SE1 3PL
020 7234 9330
bellphillips.com

Carl Trenfield Architects
11A Roper Yard
Roper Road
Canterbury CT2 7ER
01227 785768
carltrenfieldarchitects.com

Carl Turner Architects
53 Brixton Station Road
London SW9 8JH
020 7274 2902
ct-architects.co.uk

Carmody Groarke
62–70 Shorts Gardens
London WC2H 9AH
020 7836 2333
carmodygroarke.com

CarverHaggard
Unit 209
241–251 Ferndale Road
London SW9 8BJ
020 7274 2137
carverhaggard.com

Casper Mueller Kneer Architects
Podium Level
Shakespeare Tower
Barbican
London EC2Y 8DR
020 7374 2682
cmk-architects.com

Cassion Castle Architects
Studio 6c
Thane Works
London N7 7NU
020 7700 4584
cassioncastle.com

Citizens Design Bureau
Hackney Downs Studios
Amhurst Terrace
London E8 2BT
020 3095 9732
citizensdesignbureau.net

Civic Architects
142 Wood Vale
London SE23 3EB
07718 861387 & 07971 172250
civic.org.uk

Coffey Architects
11–12 Great Sutton Street
London EC1V 0BX
020 7549 2141
coffeyarchitects.com

Coombs Jones
1 Wellfield Court
Marshfield
Cardiff CF3 2TJ
07740 145400
coombsjones.com

Dallas Pierce Quintero
Studio NS22
Netil House
1 Westgate Street
London E8 3RL
020 8088 1880
dp-q.com

David Kohn Architects
Bedford House
125–133 Camden High Street
London NW1 7JR
020 7424 8596
davidkohn.co.uk

Delvendahl Martin Architects
Unit CG1
183 Bow Road
London E3 2SJ
020 7253 5963
dm-architects.co.uk

Denizen Works Ltd
29 Wadeson Street
London E2 9DR
020 3696 6900
07739 517938
denizenworks.com

DK-CM Ltd
Unit 10
5 Durham Yard
Teesdale Street
London E2 6QF
020 7729 4140
dk-cm.com

Dominic McKenzie Architects
1st Floor
9–17 St Alban's Place
London N1 0NX
020 3327 4780
dominicmckenzie.co.uk

Duggan Morris Architects Ltd
Unit 7
16–24 Underwood Street
London N1 7JQ
020 7566 7440
dugganmorrisarchitects.com

Dyvik Kahlen Architects
Unit 1
14–16 Meredith Street
London EC1R 0AB
020 3411 8434
dyvikkahlen.com

Emulsion
6 Baker's Yard
London EC1R 3DD
020 8127 1015
emulsionarchitecture.com

Erect Architecture
22b Regent Studios
8 Andrews Road
London E8 4QN
020 7254 6336
erectarchitecture.co.uk

Feilden Fowles
96 Teesdale Street
London E2 6PU
020 7033 4594
feildenfowles.co.uk

Friend and Company Architects
Unit 167
Foundling Court
The Brunswick Centre
London WC1N 1AN
020 7713 7593
friendandcompany.co.uk

Gatti Routh Rhodes Architects
Unit 1
305 Cambridge Heath Road
London E2 9LH
020 3633 3106
grr-architects.com

Gort Scott
The Print House
18 Ashwin Street
London E8 3DL
020 7254 6294
gortscott.com

Graeme Massie Architects
9–10 St Andrew Square
Edinburgh EH2 2AF
0131 556 9911
graememassie.com

Hall McKnight
Unit LM.07.0G2
11/13 Weston Street
London SE1 3ER
020 3567 1240

B111 Portview
310 Newtownards Road
Belfast BT4 1HE
028 9046 9400
hallmcknight.com

Haptic Architects
74–77 White Lion Street
London N1 9PF
020 7099 2933
hapticarchitects.com

HAT Projects Ltd
1a Mercantile House
Sir Isaac's Walk
Colchester CO1 1JJ
01206 766585
hatprojects.com

Hayhurst and Co
26 Fournier Street
London E1 6QE
020 7247 7028
hayhurstand.co.uk

Hugh Strange Architects
210 Evelyn St
London SE8 5BZ
020 8691 0494
hughstrange.com

Hugo Hardy Architect
8–12 Clarence Road Depot
Clarence Road
Berkhamsted HP4 3AS
07881 428701
hugohardyarchitect.com

Invisible Studio
Moonshine
The Rocks
Marshfield
Bath SN14 8AP
01225 287505
invisiblestudio.org

Jack Woolley
38 Thornhill Square
London N1 1BE
07773 325688
jackwoolley.co.uk

Jan Kattein Architects
277 New North Road
London N1 7AA
020 7704 0604
jankattein.com

Jonathan Hendry Architects
10 Nickerson Way
Peacefields Business Park
Holton le Clay
Lincolnshire DN36 5HS
01472 828320
jonathanhendryarchitects.com

The Building Centre
Store Street
London WC1E 7BT
020 3174 2472

Laura Dewe Mathews
104 Balcorne Street
London E9 7AU
020 8986 8926
lauradewemathews.com

Liddicoat & Goldhill LLP
Studio 6
13 Ramsgate Street
London E8 2FD
020 7923 2737
liddicoatgoldhill.com

Lyndon Goode Architects Ltd
7 Cliff Road Studios
London NW1 9AN
020 7916 1920
lyndongoode.com

Matheson Whiteley
Unit 17
38–50 Pritchards Road
London E2 9AP
020 7033 3589
mathesonwhiteley.com

Mikhail Riches
11 Clerkenwell Green
London EC1R 0DP
020 7608 1505
mikhailriches.com

MW Architects
Fifth Floor
Magdalen House
136–148 Tooley Street
London SE1 2TU
020 7407 6767
mwarchitects.co.uk

Nex
Florin Court Studios
6–9 Charterhouse Square
London EC1M 6EY
020 7183 0900
nex-architecture.com

Nissen Richards Studio
Unit 3 Waterhouse
8 Orsman Road
London N1 5QJ
020 7870 8899
nissenrichardsstudio.com

OMMX Architects
Studio E2S
Cockpit Arts
Northington Street
London WC1N 2NP
020 7405 5484
officemmx.com

Ordinary Architecture
Winkley Street Studios
7 Winkley Street
London E2 6PY
020 7729 4311
ordinaryarchitecture.co.uk

Orkidstudio
5 Newton Place
Glasgow G3 7PR
07795 097175
orkidstudio.co.uk

OS31 Architects
Studio 9
The Cube
1 Brittain Street
Sheffield S1 4RJ
0114 213 0065
os31.net

Platform 5 Architects LLP
Unit 102
94 Hanbury Street
London E1 5JL
020 7377 8885
platform5architects.com

Practice Architecture
16 Wild's Rents
London SE1 4QG
07738 308058 (Paloma Gormley)
07828 920235 (Lettice Drake)
practicearchitecture.co.uk

Prewett Bizley Architects
Beacon View
Peak Lane
Compton Dundon
Somerset TA11 6NZ
01458 273778

Second Floor
118a London Wall
London EC2Y 5JA
020 7256 2195
prewettbizley.com

Pricegore
Studio A4A
Copeland Business Park
133 Copeland Road
London SE15 3SN
07973 218514 (Dingle Price)
07862 254395 (Alex Gore)
pricegore.co.uk

PUP Architects
32 Woodlea Road
London N16 0TH
hello@puparchitects.com
puparchitects.com

RA Projects
No. 24
60 Shepherdess Walk
London N1 7QZ
rashid@rashidali.eu
raprojects.info

RCKa
29–31 Cowper St
London EC2A 4AT
020 7831 7002
rcka.co.uk

Robin Lee Architecture
71 Queensway
London W2 4QH
020 3368 6724
robinleearchitecture.com

3 Clanwilliam Terrace
Grand Canal Quay
Dublin 2

Roz Barr Architects Ltd
111–113 St John Street
London EC1V 4JA
020 7253 5336
rozbarr.com

Rural Office For Architecture
Pantybara
Felindre
Llandysul SA44 5XT
01559 505008

70 Cowcross Street
London EC1M 6EJ
07710 572562
ruralofficeforarchitecture.co.uk

Russian for Fish
Unit 5
Durham Yard
5 Teesdale Street
London E2 6QF
020 7739 4442
russianforfish.com

Sam Jacob Studio Ltd
5 Rear Thornhill Road
London N1 1HX
020 7251 6735
samjacob.com

Sandy Rendel Architects Ltd
Unit 7S
Vanguard Court
Rear of 36–38 Peckham Road
London SE5 8QT
020 3602 1260
sandyrendel.com

Serie Architects
Unit 2P
Leroy House
436 Essex Road
London N1 3QP
020 7226 0022
serie.co.uk

Something & Son
20 Dalston Lane
London E8 3AZ
someone@somethingandson.com
somethingandson.com

Stitch
Unit 11
The Dove Centre
109 Bartholomew Road
London NW5 2BJ
020 3617 8725
stitch-studio.co.uk

Studio Egret West
3 Brewhouse Yard
London EC1V 4JQ
020 7549 1730
egretwest.com

Studio Gil Ltd
116 Liverpool Road
London N1 0RE
020 7617 7932
studio-gil.com

Studio Sam Causer
13 Princes Street
Margate CT9 1PF
020 7193 7289
samcauser.com

Studio Weave
109b Mare Street Studios
203–213 Mare Street
Hackney E8 3QE
020 7099 1922
studioweave.com

Surman Weston Ltd
Studio S2
23–27 Arcola Street
London E8 2DJ
020 3816 0242
surmanweston.com

Takero Shimazaki Architects
6a Peacock Yard
Iliffe Street
London SE17 3LH
020 7928 9171
t-sa.co.uk

TDO Architecture
80 Great Suffolk Street
London SE1 0BE
020 7928 8787
tdoarchitecture.com

The Klassnik Corporation
Studio 12
80a Ashfield Street
London E1 2BJ
020 8819 3243
klassnik.com

Timothy Smith &
Jonathan Taylor LLP
Studio B.209
Lighthouse Studios
89a Shacklewell Lane
London E8 2EB
020 7241 1494
smithandtaylorllp.com

Urban Projects Bureau
Room 1
Malvern House
15 & 16 Nassau Street
London W1W 7AB
020 3581 7370
urbanprojectsbureau.com

VPPR Architects
Unit 12
5 Durham Yard
London E2 6QF
020 7729 6168
vppr.co.uk

We Made That LLP
30–32 Stamford Road
London N1 4JL
020 7249 6336
wemadethat.co.uk

West Architecture
3 Greenland Place
Camden
London NW1 0AP
020 7482 6849
westarchitecture.co.uk

William Matthews Associates
10 Clerkenwell Green
London EC1R 0DP
020 7566 0071
wma.co

William Smalley
The Dairy
40 Emerald Street
London WC1N 3NG
020 7242 0028
williamsmalley.com

YOU&ME
Unit 802 Verdigris
31 Old Bethnal Green Road
London E2 6AA
020 3287 3533
youandmearchitecture.com

Picture credits

Friend and Company
p144 Agnese Sanvito; p145 (top) Adam Dawe; p145 (below) Ioana Marinescu.

Gatti Routh Rhodes Architects
p146 Lyubomira Lyubenova.

Gort Scott
p148–151 David Grandorge.

Graeme Massie Architects
p152 Graeme Massie Architects; p153 (below left) David Stewart Photography.

Hall McKnight
p157 (below),158–9 Donal McCann; p161 Stamers Kontor.

HAT Projects
p164, 165 (top), 167 Ioana Marinescu; p165 (below), 166 (left) HAT Projects; p166 (right) Hugo Glendinning.

Hayhurst and Co
p168, 169 (top), 170 (top), 171 Kilian O'Sullivan.

Hugh Strange Architects
p172, 173 (below left & right), 175, 176–177 David Grandorge; p173 (top), 174 Hugh Strange Architects.

Hugo Hardy Architect
p178, 179 Hugo Hardy.

Invisible Studio
p180, 181 Valerie Bennett; p182 Peter Cook; p183 Andy Matthews.

Jack Woolley
p184, 185 Jack Woolley.

Jonathan Hendry Architects
p188–190 David Grandorge.

Laura Dewe Mathews
p192, 193 (top & below left) Chloe Dewe Mathews; p193 (below right) Ed Reeve.

Lyndon Goode Architects
p196 Simona Mizzoni/Lyndon Goode Architects; p197 (top left & below) Lyndon Goode Architects; p197 (top right) Ava Richardson/Lyndon Goode Architects.

Matheson Whiteley
p198 Matheson Whiteley; p199 Maris Mezulis.

Mikhail Riches
p200, 201 Tim Crocker; p202 Mark Hadden.

MW Architects
p204 Ben Blossom; p205 French + Tye.

Nex
p207 James Brittain.

Nissen Richards Studio
p208 David Lambert; p209 Tom Merrell.

Ordinary Architecture
p212 Carl Glover.

Orkidstudio
p214 Orkidstudio; p215 Peter Didbin; p216–217 Odysseas Mourtzouchos.

OS31 Architects
p218, 219 OS31.

Platform 5 Architects
p220 Alan Williams Photography; p221 Platform 5 Architect.

Practice Architecture
p222 Damian Griffiths. p224–225 Richard Bryant

Prewett Bizley
p226 Kilian O'Sullivan/VIEW; p227 Graham Bizley.

Pricegore
p228, 229 Ioana Marinescu.

RA Projects
p232 Lyndon Douglas.

RCKa
p234, 238 RCKa; p235, 236–237, 239 (below) Jakob Spriestersbach; p239 (top) Ivan Jones.

Robin Lee Architecture
p240, 241 Andrew Lee; p242 James Newton.

Roz Barr Architects
p244 Andrew Putler; p245 (top) John MacLean; p246 Matt Chisnell.

Rural Office for Architecture
p249 Rural Office for Architecture.

Russian for Fish
p250 Gareth Gardner; p251 (bottom) Peter Landers.

Sandy Rendel Architects
p255 (bottom) Sandy Rendel Architects.

Serie Architects
p256–258, 259 (below) Serie Architects; p258 Serie Architects/ Fram Petit; p259 (top) Serie Architects/MIR.

Something & Son
p260 Courtesy PJ Rankin; p261 (top left) Andy Merritt; p261 (top right and below) Patrick Wack.

Studio Egret West
p264, 265 Urban Splash; p266–267 Matt Clayton; p268 Gareth Gardner.

Studio Gil
p270 Fernando Agreda; p271 Simon Kennedy.

Studio Sam Causer
p272, 273 Studio Sam Causer.

Studio Weave
p274, 275 Johnny Barrington.

Surman Weston
p280, 281, 283 Wai Ming Ng.

Takero Shimazaki Architects
p286 Helene Binet.

TDO Architecture
p286, 287 Ben Blossom.

The Klassnik Corporation
p289 Guy Archard.

Urban Projects Bureau
p292 Kilian O'Sullivan; p293 Richard Leeney.

VPPR
p294 Noel Read; p295 Hélène Binet.

We Made That
p296 Jakob Spriestersbach; p297 We Made That.

West Architecture
p298 Ben Blossom; p299 Peter Cook.

William Matthews Associates
p301 (right) Nick Wood (photography); p301 (right) Hayes Davidson (visualization).

William Smalley
p302 Alex James; p303 Hélène Binet.

YOU&ME
p304, 305 YOU&ME.

Sponsors' comments

The last 10 years, the epoch of the 'post-digital age' – or, as some call it, the 'second machine age' – has been a roller coaster for those of us engaged in design. We have all grappled with the question of how to ensure a sustainable future for independent practice in a landscape dominated by large-scale multidisciplinary firms with access to many sectors and countries. Discussion of the merits of size is prone to result in contradictions, clichés and credulous repetition; the future of architecture remains in the hands of practices of the scale and talent included in this publication.

At AKT II, we have been fortunate to engage with many of them, both in practice and education. We consistently see the confidence, enthusiasm and restraint they bring to the task of creating value for their clients, without compromising their individuality. Their interaction with engineers and many other design disciplines reinforces their work, and frequently pushes us to reconsider how we practice. Looking at the diverse work included in this book, what is particularly impressive is the extent to which this generation has gone beyond the possibilities of new digital technologies, recognising that software can never be a surrogate for an intellectual position or design excellence.

Hanif Kara is a Trustee of the Architecture Foundation and founding director of the structural engineers, AKT II

When choosing an architect, developers need to match them to the requirements of the site. Each project has a unique set of requirements determined by location, use and scale. However, the unifying skill set for delivering great architecture – for both architect and developer – is a strong vision, a desire to push the boundaries and the ability and willingness to come on a journey, which often spans many years. From my experience, there are no easy straightforward projects and smaller buildings require just as much careful thinking as skyscrapers.

It is fantastic for any developer to work with established and renowned architects. However, developers should not dismiss smaller practises. I've found young architects bring an enormous amount of passion to the project. They tend to offer creative and new insights and are willing to find innovative solutions to practical issues, like costs and budgets.

Diversity in age, gender and culture within architectural practices provide the key to a thorough understanding of the complex aspects behind a successfully designed building. How we go about our daily lives and how we use space has changed hugely and will continue to do so. Today's design needs to strive to find the right answers by addressing problems the user didn't even think they had. This new generation of architects bring fresh insight into responding to these challenges. What's fundamentally important is selecting a creative team that demonstrates commitment, dedication and shares the same ambition of making a difference.

Almacantar is delighted to support the New Architects 3 book, which recognises the rising stars in the industry. As a business we are committed to identifying and rewarding emerging talent. Nurturing new talent, by taking a chance with a lesser know firm, is one of the most rewarding decisions a business can make. You never know, you might have just appointed a future Stirling Prize winner!

Kathrin Hersel is development director of property investment and development company Almacantar

I can still recall the importance to the four founding partners when, in 1994, we were informed that we were to be included in the Architecture Foundation's exhibition and publication, New British Architecture.

The Architecture Foundation and ourselves were fledgling organisations, but very different ones. Allford Hall Monaghan Morris was a new practice with small projects. The AF, by contrast, had a gravitas bestowed by the ambitions and status of the founding Director and Trustees, its magnificent location in the base of the Economist tower and the fact that, beyond the architecture schools, it was the sole light in an architectural scene much less crowded than today.

The early days of a practice are always the toughest as your raison d'être is being both defined, and in doubt: what use is an architectural position when there is no work and the focus moves to survival? Of course it was ever thus. So even the most resolute are buoyed by the imprimatur of peer recognition. Our inclusion in the first New British Architecture book, the exhibition and legendary launch party were certainly a defining moment for fellow travellers and ourselves. So we very much hope that this new publication gives sustenance and succour to the very talented practices included and that it helps them to construct new opportunities to make their particular architecture.

Over twenty years on, this new publication is a timely reminder that in architecture, it is better to travel hopefully than ever to arrive!

Simon Allford is chairman of the Architecture Foundation Trustees and founding director of Allford Hall Monaghan Morris Architects

There is a real hunger for the critical thinking and fresh creative surge of ideas illustrated and recorded in the work of the generation of practices chosen for New Architects 3. Inevitably the old established guard gets weary, complacent and forgetful of the intense debate that accompanies the sowing of ideas in schools of architecture, evident for instance in the Architecture Foundation's Futures in the Making, an exhibition that celebrated the rich diversity of opinion and expanding means of representation available to architectural students today.

It takes a number of years, perhaps even a couple of decades, before those hard won ideas bear fruit in the thrill of experiencing their realisation and that is what this timely book celebrates. In all the din of architectural publication this book will rise in retrospect to be seen as a very important imprint for today and promise of a more resourceful, reflective and ethically grounded architecture practice tomorrow.

Eric Parry is a Trustee of the Architecture Foundation and founding director of Eric Parry Architects

Acknowledgments

The Architecture Foundation would like to thank the following sponsors, organisations and individuals who have generously contributed to the success of this project:

Sponsors Hanif Kara, AKT II; Allford Hall Monaghan Morris Architects; Almacantar; Eric Parry Architects.

Selection panel Pamela Buxton, architecture and design writer; Kate Goodwin, head of architecture at the Royal Academy; Edwin Heathcote, architecture and design critic of the Financial Times; Catherine Slessor, architecture and design writer; Oliver Wainwright, architecture and design critic of The Guardian; Vicky Richardson, director of architecture, design and fashion at the British Council.

Special thanks Sarah Gaventa, Teresa Lima, Hugh Merrell

Practice texts and captioning Pamela Buxton

Graphic Design John Morgan Studio

The Architecture Foundation

Trustees Simon Allford, director of Allford Hall Monaghan Morris (chair); Tom Dyckhoff, critic and broadcaster; Hanif Kara, director of AKT II; Farshid Moussavi, director of Farshid Moussavi Architecture; Professor Robert Mull, dean and director of The Cass; Eric Parry, director of Eric Parry Architects; Peter Rees, professor of Places and City Planning, the Bartlett; Bettina von Hase, director of Nine AM; Matthew White, partner of Herbert Smith Freehills.

Director Ellis Woodman
Deputy Director Phineas Harper
Operations Manager Matea Vlaskalic

architecturefoundation.org.uk

almacantar

Eric Parry Architects

ALLFORD
HALL
MONAGHAN
MORRIS

First published 2016 by Merrell Publishers,
London and New York

Merrell Publishers Limited
70 Cowcross Street
London EC1M 6EJ
merrellpublishers.com

in association with

The Architecture Foundation
The Cass
London Metropolitan University
Central House
50–63 Whitechapel High Street
London E1 7PF
architecturefoundation.org.uk

Designed by John Morgan studio
Produced by Merrell Publishers Limited

Printed and bound in China

British Library Cataloguing in Publication Data.
A catalogue record for this book is available from
the British Library.

ISBN 978-1-8589-4645-0